TALES FROM THE

PITTSBURGH PENGUINS

Joe Starkey

SP
SPORTS
PUBLISHING
L.L.C.

SportsPublishingLLC.com

ISBN-10: 1-58261-199-8
ISBN-13: 978-1-58261-199-0

Publishers: Peter L. Bannon and Joseph J. Bannon Sr.
Senior managing editor: Susan M. Moyer
Acquisitions editor: John Humenik
Developmental editor: Mark Newton
Art director: K. Jeffrey Higgerson
Dust jacket design: Dustin Hubbart
Project manager: Kathryn R. Holleman
Photo editor: Erin Linden-Levy

Sports Publishing L.L.C.
804 North Neil Street
Champaign, IL 61820
Phone: 1-877-424-2665
Fax: 217-363-2073
SportsPublishingLLC.com

Printed in the United States of America

Library of Congress Cataloging-in-Publication Data

Starkey, Joe, 1965-
    Tales from the Pittsburgh Penguins / Joe Starkey.
      p. cm.
    ISBN-13: 978-1-58261-199-0 (hard cover : alk. paper)
    ISBN-10: 1-58261-199-8 (hard cover : alk. paper)
    1. Pittsburgh Penguins (Hockey team)--History. 2. Pittsburgh Penguins (Hockey team)--Anecdotes. I. Title.
GV848.P58S73 2007
796.962'640974886--dc22
                                              2006029595

TO MY FATHER, WHO INSTILLED IN ME A LOVE OF STORIES.

CONTENTS

FOREWORD

A lot of the kids who come along today don't have an appreciation of how this all came to be and who traveled the path before them. I think it's important to have a sense of history—in this case, the Pittsburgh Penguins' history.

There are so many great moments, so many special moments. Here, you have a chance to see and hear and feel what happened with this franchise in the early days all the way through the Stanley Cup years and beyond.

You know, everybody has their day, sooner or later.

I remember all the commercial travel we had to do and the crazy, funny, wonderful things that went on, the comical parts of being together all the time in such a public atmosphere.

I remember guys playing jokes on people in the airport. Gilles Lupien would tie a five-dollar bill on a string, and the guys would sit and watch as people walked by. Most would not try to pick it up. If they did, Gilles would pull the string, and the whole place would erupt.

One day, a guy grabbed the money and said, "I'm keeping it," and walked off. It was a ten-dollar bill that time, and that was a lot of money in those days.

I think Gilles used a one-dollar bill on his next escapade.

Joe Starkey—the man who wrote this book, not the fellow by the same name whom I replaced as the team's radio voice in 1974—has compiled a collection of many such stories. Joe has a real appreciation of the game, a real sense of hockey history, and there aren't many harder working human beings.

He learned the game from the ground up, and there's a beauty in that. I did the same thing. I hadn't seen a game until I was 20. Fortunately, I had some very good teachers.

You'll meet a few of them on the pages that follow—and if you're like I was when I read this book, you'll be "smiling like a butcher's dog!"

Enjoy.

—Mike Lange

1

THE EARLY YEARS

(1967-1974)

SKATING NUNS

The former Carol Dangerfield, wife of a team investor, gave Pittsburgh's NHL expansion club its nickname in 1967. For all the respect the name garnered, it might as well have come from Rodney Dangerfield.

The Pittsburgh *Penguins?*

Publicity director Joe Gordon was flabbergasted. He had to announce the name during a dinner at the swanky Pittsburgh Athletic Association.

People laughed.

"Can you imagine trying to promote a team whose nickname is the Penguins?" Gordon said later. "A penguin isn't the most graceful animal on the face of the earth. It waddles."

Head coach George "Red" Sullivan wasn't thrilled with the name, either.

"I can see it now," Sullivan told reporters. "The day after we play a bad game, the sportswriters will say, 'They skated like a bunch of nuns.'"

Officially, the team was named on February 10, 1967, after it fielded more than 26,000 entries from a newspaper contest. It even drew a winner, but the truth is that Carol McGregor, wife of investor John McGregor, came up with the name Penguins because she liked the alliteration, the possibility of black-and-white uniforms (it didn't happen) and the notion of penguins playing in the Igloo, the popular name for Pittsburgh's Civic Arena.

General manager Jack Riley was partial to the name Shamrocks, seeing as he and fellow Irishman Sullivan were running the show (and there had been a team called the Pittsburgh Shamrocks in the International Hockey League in the 1930s). Others favored Hornets, after Pittsburgh's championship minor-league team. Eskimos received consideration, too, but this team would be called the Penguins, a name quickly shortened to "Pens" in local vernacular.

A couple of decades later, the name took on new significance—and gained several measures of respect—when the Penguins were twice crowned league champions.

"I didn't think a hell of a lot of the name," Sullivan said later. "But it turned out to be OK."

DEATH OF A MASCOT

The Penguins' first mascot took the ice before games at the beginning of the 1968-69 season. There wasn't much glitter to his act.

"He just kind of waddled out and waddled off," goaltender Les Binkley said of Pete the Penguin, an Ecuadorian-born bird on loan from the Pittsburgh Zoo.

Average attendance that season was a franchise record-low 6,008, but Pete was well-loved—and much grieved when he died of pneumonia two months into the season.

Some of the players heard that Pete had been mishandled.

"He was a penguin, an animal, and they wanted to keep him warm," recalled defenseman Duane Rupp. "Well, he didn't want to be warm. He wanted to be cold."

"I remember that he died and that they brought in another one," Binkley said. "They called the second one 'Re-Pete.'"

BUILDING FROM SCRATCH

The Penguins have spent a good part of their history trying to find ways to compete against better-financed and bigger-market teams. It was true from the very start of the franchise, in 1967, when general manager Jack Riley faced the prospect of building a competitive club from the scrap heap.

Expansion had doubled the National Hockey League from six teams to 12, and there were precious few talented players available in the amateur draft because established teams owned junior clubs and had rights to the players.

Also, the original six teams were allowed to protect their top 11 players for the expansion draft and one of every two players after that. As a capper, two of the six new expansion teams—Philadelphia and Los Angeles—literally bought minor-league teams with ready-made talent.

"They got the jump on us, and they finished 1-2 in the division," Riley said, adding that all six expansion teams were put into the same division.

Riley was under pressure to form a competitive team immediately, because Pittsburgh's minor-league club, the Hornets, had won the Calder Cup championship the year before. That was the Hornets' final season.

"Pittsburgh was used to seeing a winner," Riley said.

Riley signed nine former Hornets that first season. The team's payroll was $315,000. Six years later, the Buffalo Sabres would sign star center Gilbert Perreault for more than that.

"Nobody can accuse me of not being frugal," Riley said.

Andy Bathgate, 35, was the Penguins' highest-paid player at $25,000, or less than what today's stars make in a single game. Riley drew the same salary.

"We were strapped for money," coach George "Red" Sullivan recalled. "And the Hornets were a tough act to follow, but I had a good bunch of guys who rallied around each other."

The Penguins finished just two points out of a playoff spot that season. They also had a penalty-killing percentage of 83.9, which would remain the franchise's high-water mark for 29 years.

LAST RITES

How tough was the Penguins' first coach, George "Red" Sullivan? Well, during his playing days, he was administered last rites after Montreal defenseman Doug Harvey speared him so hard he ruptured Sullivan's spleen.

In those days, teams would often play each other on back-to-back nights. Sullivan played for the Rangers, and on a Saturday in Montreal, he kicked the skates from under Harvey, who looked up and said, "I'll get you tomorrow, Sullivan."

The next night in New York, Harvey followed through on his threat. Sullivan went down. He got up and tried to play, but finally said, "I can't go." He was sent to a nearby hospital in a cab.

"I can remember the priest and the doctors standing around me," Sullivan said. "I was pretty sick."

He and Harvey never spoke about the incident. Harvey later played for Pittsburgh's Calder Cup–winning American Hockey League team, the Hornets.

TWO-MILLION-DOLLAR MAN

Joe Gordon, the Penguins' original publicity director, felt like a rich man when he accompanied team management to NHL headquarters in Montreal in June of 1967. That is where the Pittsburgh Penguins were announced as part of the NHL's six-team expansion. Gordon was carrying the team's $2 million entry fee in the form of a check.

"It was kind of exhilarating, even though it wasn't my money and there was nothing I could do with it," Gordon said. "To me, the most incredible thing looking back was that a franchise cost only $2 million."

CLEARING THE TRACK

Former Penguins general manager Jack Riley isn't proud of the fact that he traded Rene Robert—a future member of Buffalo's famed "French Connection"—for aging winger Eddie Shack late in the 1971-72 season. But at least Pittsburgh got some serious entertainment value out of the deal.

There was nothing quite like a Shack-led rush. At 6-foot-1, 200 pounds, he was one of the league's bigger forwards, if not one of the more graceful ones.

"I used to tee it up for him and get out of there in a hurry," recalled goaltender Les Binkley. "He'd wind up and go behind the net, arms and legs and everything flailing."

Back in Toronto, when Shack played for the Maple Leafs, they used to say, "Clear the Track, here comes Eddie Shack!"

Legend has it that Shack couldn't read or write. When he played for the Maple Leafs, he'd heard that Detroit coach Jack Adams criticized him for not being able to spell. So when Shack scored against the Red Wings in the next game, he skated by the Detroit bench and said, "Hey, Jack: G-O-A-L.'"

In Pittsburgh, coach Leonard "Red" Kelly would write practice times on a blackboard.

Clear the track! Eddie Shack moves in on Vancouver Canucks goalie Dunc Wilson.
(Photo courtesy of the Pittsburgh Penguins)

"One time Red put on the blackboard, 'No practice tomorrow,'"
Binkley said. "Eddie was the only guy who showed up."

On power plays, Shack would jump over the boards and say to his
coach, 'OK, Leonard, who are the other four guys?'"

It wasn't as if Shack couldn't play. He had 25 goals in his only full
season with the Penguins.

DUNE BUGGY

Eddie Shack used to drive a Dune Buggy with his No. 23 painted
on the hood. One morning while nobody in authority was watching,
he drove it into the Civic Arena, right through the gates, right onto
the ice.

"I looked, and he came wheeling down the ramp," recalled
equipment man John Doolan. "He started doing wheelies, and he
nearly took out the end boards."

FASHION STATEMENT

It was believed that Jack Riley, the Penguins' first general manager, came up with the team's original colors of Colombia blue, Navy blue and white.

True?

"I'm guilty," Riley said.

Riley was from Toronto, where he followed the Argonauts of the Canadian Football League. They also used double shades of blue.

"Our light blue turned out too babyish blue," he said.

A local freelance artist named Bob Gessner designed the original logo featuring the skating penguin wearing a scarf in front of a gold triangle—symbolic of the city's Golden Triangle—but it was never used on a jersey, only on pucks and team letterhead. Publicity director Joe Gordon had the idea of putting a penguin on the Golden Triangle.

Sullivan, a former Rangers player, urged the team to use the diagonal "Pittsburgh" font, similar to the one the Rangers used. Ticket prices for home games at the Civic Arena in the Penguins' first season were $5, $4, $3.50 and $2.50—or about what various concessions would go for 30 years later.

THANKS, BUT NO THANKS

It seemed like an incredible opportunity for minor-league journeyman Jeannot Gilbert. A 26-year-old winger, he'd hooked on with the expansion Penguins in training camp of 1967 after several seasons with the Hershey Bears of the American Hockey League.

Two days before the season opener, just as he was about to sign a contract, Gilbert suddenly decided he wanted to go back to the minors. It didn't help that he'd taken a slash in the back of his legs during an exhibition game two nights earlier.

"I said, 'What's the matter, don't you want to play in the National Hockey League?'" GM Jack Riley remembered. "In his broken English, he said, 'No, I just like to play in Hershey.'"

Riley called Hershey boss Frank Mathers and asked if he wanted Gilbert back. Mathers said yes, because Gilbert was a talented scorer at that level. Riley asked who he could have in return.

Mathers shot back, "Who do you want?"

Riley wanted Gene Ubriaco, who scored 18 goals for the Penguins that season and years later became their coach.

This is the original Pittsburgh Penguins logo. *(Photo courtesy of the Pittsburgh Penguins)*

MAGIC BUS

If it happened today, Bryan Watson figures, "I'd be in jail."

Luckily, it happened in the early 1970s, in Los Angeles, as the Penguins boarded a Marriott courtesy bus after traveling all day. Somebody accidentally bumped the gear shift with an equipment bag, prompting Watson to jump behind the wheel to put the bus in park.

That would have been the end of it, but the bus driver—a "kid from the hotel"—reprimanded Watson, and anyone who knew the combative defenseman knew that wasn't a good idea.

This was a guy who body-checked his teammates in warmups, just to make sure they were ready.

"I got mad," Watson said. "And somebody in the back of the bus said, 'You don't have a hair on your [butt] unless you drive this thing to the hotel.'

"I said, 'If I can get this door closed, we're on our way, boys!' I was like Jackie Gleason in the *Honeymooners*.

"After I'd gone 50 feet, I realized, 'Holy Geez, I better be careful.' Everybody was going nuts, laughing, carrying on. You would have thought we were drunk, but that's the thing: We hadn't had a drink. Unfortunately, there were some regular people on the bus who were scared to death."

Once the team reached the hotel, coach Ken Schinkel called a meeting.

"He didn't want to know who did it," Watson said, "but he didn't want it to happen again, either."

CHAINSAW MASSACRE

Picking the Most Hated Penguin of all time is a near-impossible task. Darius Kasparaitis, Ulf Samuelsson, Gary Rissling, "Battleship" Bob Kelly, Rod Buskas, Dave Schultz, and many others would receive votes.

But if you asked opposing star forwards of the early 1970s, Bryan Watson might win by a landslide.

Watson, a defenseman acquired from Oakland in 1969, racked up 871 penalty minutes and at least that many resentments in only 303 games with the Penguins. Future Hall of Famers such as Gordie Howe and Bobby Hull positively despised Watson, who fed off the venom directed at him in opposing arenas.

Bryan Watson took the hotel bus for a joy ride. *(Photo courtesy of the Pittsburgh Penguins)*

Shortly after retiring, Watson nearly lost an arm in a chainsaw accident. Howe's reaction: "Oh yeah? How's the [freaking] chainsaw doing?'"

FIRST GAME

It seemed like a classic case of professional suicide when Penguins general manager Jack Riley petitioned the NHL to let his expansion team play its first game against the defending Stanley Cup-champion Montreal Canadiens.

It would mark the first time an expansion club played one of the NHL's established teams in the 12-team league, and it appeared to be a colossal mismatch.

There was a method to Riley's madness. "I figured if they could ever be taken, that was the time," he said.

It almost happened. The Canadiens escaped with a 2-1 victory on October 11, 1967, before a crowd of 9,307 (3,273 below capacity) at the Civic Arena.

"It was a hell of a hockey game," recalled Penguins coach George "Red" Sullivan.

Regal veteran Andy Bathgate, who wore a turtleneck under his jersey, scored for the Penguins, and the great Jean Beliveau scored the winner for Montreal, becoming just the third player in league history to reach the 400-goal plateau.

Afterward, legendary Montreal coach Toe Blake blasted his players.

"I never saw our team so nervous," he told reporters. "We must have given them the puck I don't know how many times. Stupid backpasses, something I've been harping on for two weeks. They proved they can still do it."

Rogie Vachon gained the victory for Montreal. He would get 33 more against the Penguins before his NHL career was finished, becoming the all-time winningest goaltender against them.

BOBBY CLARKE TO PENS?

The Penguins thought about drafting Bobby Clarke in 1969, but, like every other team, passed on the future Hall of Famer because they were concerned about his diabetes.

The Penguins instead took forgettable center Rick Kessell with the first pick of the second round (15th overall). The Philadelphia Flyers chose Clarke two picks later, after ignoring him in the first round.

How drastically would history have been altered if the Penguins had taken Clarke? Well, for one thing, they might not have gone 15 years and 42 games without a victory at the Spectrum in Philadelphia. The Flyers probably wouldn't have won two Stanley Cups, and the

Penguins would have had two dynamic players from that draft. They took 5-foot-10, 160-pound center Michel Briere 26th overall. Other teams ignored Briere because of his size. He had an outstanding rookie year in 1969-70 but died in an automobile accident that summer.

"We could have had both players," Riley said. "I've often wondered what that would have been like."

MICHEL BRIERE

Michel Briere knew how good he was, even if others had their doubts because of his smallish stature (5-foot-10, 160 pounds). The Penguins made him a third-round draft pick (26th overall) in 1969, the first year of the NHL Entry Draft, and he immediately asked for more money than they were offering.

General manager Jack Riley offered a $13,000 salary with a $4,000 signing bonus. Briere wanted a $5,000 bonus.

"I asked why," Riley recalled. "And he said, 'Because I'll be playing hockey in Pittsburgh for the next 20 years.'"

If only that pledge had come true. Two weeks after his marvelous rookie season—and three weeks before he was to be married—Briere sustained fatal injuries when his burnt-orange, 1970 Cougar failed to negotiate a curve on Highway 117 near his home in Malartic, Quebec. He was with two friends. It never was determined who was behind the wheel.

Ever the competitor, Briere held on for 11 months in a coma before he died on April 13, 1971, leaving behind a son, Martin.

"That was a big part of our franchise," Riley said.

Tragically, the ambulance that picked up Briere killed an 18-year-old bicyclist on the way to the hospital.

"It was one of Briere's friends," Riley said.

Riley and others visited Briere often as he lay in a hospital bed.

"I'd grab his hand and I'd say, 'Let's go, Mike, we've got to play St. Louis tonight'—that was our biggest rival—and he'd grab my hand tight," Riley said. "But as the visits went on, there was no communication at all."

Briere was third on the team in scoring that season, with 44 points (12 goals, 32 assists). He raised his game in the playoffs, leading the team in scoring with eight points. The Penguins finished just two victories short of the Stanley Cup final, losing to St. Louis in the semifinals.

Michel Briere died tragically after an outstanding rookie season.
(Photo courtesy of the Pittsburgh Penguins)

"He was quite slight and small but very shifty and fast," recalled teammate Ron Schock. "He had a great attitude. I sat beside him in the dressing room. He was a real nice young kid. I liked him very much."

The number 21 already held esteemed status in Pittsburgh because it was worn by Pirates Hall of Fame outfielder Roberto Clemente, who, like Briere, died young.

About a week before the accident, Riley had spoken with Briere at a team function. Briere wanted a salary bump in year two, from $13,000 to $18,000.

"I knew he was worth it," Riley said. "I told him, 'We'll see in the fall.'"

WANT TO BUY A HOCKEY TEAM?

George Steinbrenner once had an interest in buying the Penguins. So did famous singer Andy Williams.

There were a whole bunch of other folks who actually went through with the idea . . . and were sorry they did. Nothing reflects the team's roller-coaster history more than the long line of men who've sunk money into what has been a shaky proposition from day one.

Actually, before day one. A group of 21 owners invested $2 million to get the Penguins started in 1967. General manager Jack Riley remembered a request being made to hold the check a few extra days, just so more interest could be collected.

Many of the same owners had invested in a soccer team called the Pittsburgh Phantoms, which played before miniscule crowds at Forbes Field and lost about $700,000 before the Penguins opened for business.

The Penguins' original publicity director, Joe Gordon, remembered that Peter Block, one of the Penguins' first investors, was convinced soccer represented the cutting edge of North American sports and would prove to be a money maker.

Gordon had his doubts about the Phantoms and the Penguins.

"You knew it was shaky because they had so many investors," he said. "You had a lot of guys who didn't have a lot of cash lying around."

Five months into the Penguins' first season, they were sold. Detroit banker Donald Parsons bought 80 percent of the team and started throwing money around. He promised each of his players in 1969-70 a $400 bonus if the team finished third or better in the Western Division. It did. He paid. But he soon was spent himself.

This would be a repeated theme among Penguins' owners.

"I really don't know all the ramifications," Riley said. "But I know this: When we went to the draft the first year Parsons was here, he picked me up in his private plane. The next year, we had to send him a plane ticket to Montreal, because the league was going to run the team."

The league did indeed run the team during the 1970-71 season, while Parson solicited offers. Before one game that season, Penguins defenseman Bryan Watson skated past NHL president Clarence Campbell and said, "Clarence, 'How's your team doing tonight?'"

BEER FOR BINK

Long before Eddie Johnston became a fixture in the Penguins organization, he was a popular goaltender for the Boston Bruins, and he treated his fellow goalies with the utmost respect.

Which is to say, he gave them beer.

After each game, the opposing goalie could find a six-pack in a bucket of ice with a towel over it, courtesy of "E.J."

That six-pack turned into a 12-pack for Penguins goalie Les Binkley on January 28, 1968, at the Boston Garden. In one of the more memorable performances in team history, Binkley made 33 saves in a 1-0 shutout, one of six he recorded that season. Most of his saves were of the spectacular variety against the most intimidating offensive machine in hockey.

The Penguins were dreadfully outplayed, but Binkley turned aside everything that Bobby Orr, Phil Esposito, Ken Hodge, Johnny Bucyk & Co. had to offer.

"It was one of those nights you couldn't do anything wrong," recalled Binkley, the Penguins' very first player.

Johnston didn't play that night—Gerry Cheevers tended goal for Boston—so he had a rink-side seat for Binkley's show.

"I don't think we flooded the ice in our end that night," Johnston said. "I sent a note that said, 'Bink, I know I usually send you six, but tonight I think you'll need a dozen.' We took care of each other."

Little-known defenseman George Konik scored the only goal in the game, thus becoming the answer to a trivia question. Konik is the answer to another trivia question, as well. He scored the first penalty-shot goal for the franchise, January 31, 1968, at St. Louis against legendary goaltender Glenn Hall.

SAVING FACE (OR NOT)

During the summers, Andy Brown loved to race dirt-track cars. During the season, he loved to face speeding pucks. And he did so without the benefit of a goalie mask.

In fact, on April 7, 1974, in a 6-3 loss to the Atlanta Flames, Brown became the last NHL goaltender to play a game without a shred of facial protection. This was a full 15 years after Toronto's Jacques Plante made history by becoming the first goalie to don a mask.

"Oh geez, Andy was a different guy, to say the least," recalled teammate Bryan Watson. "But he was a real competitor."

There were no limits on stick curves in those days, so shots often went wildly off target. Watson remembered seeing another

Andy Brown was the last NHL goalie to play a game without a mask.
(Photo courtesy of the Pittsburgh Penguins)

goaltender, Gump Worsley, drop like a wounded elephant after absorbing a Bobby Hull slap shot to the ear.

"Hull shot it 100 mph," Watson said.

Plante first donned a mask on November 1, 1959, after a shot from New York Ranger—and future Penguin—Andy Bathgate cut him in the face.

The feisty Brown had 60 penalty minutes, fifth on the team, in 1973-74, which was his only full season. He signed with the WHAs Indianapolis Racers that summer. The historic game against the Flames proved to be the last of his NHL career.

MONEY ON THE FLOOR

In their third season (1969-70) the Penguins finished 12 games under .500 but made an unlikely run at the Stanley Cup, falling just two victories short of the final. They wouldn't get that close again for more than 20 years.

Their new coach was Hall of Famer Leonard "Red" Kelly, who'd learned a thing or two about motivating players during his playing career, when he was part of eight Cup-winning teams.

During the playoffs that year, Kelly borrowed a ploy he'd seen from legendary Toronto Maple Leafs coach Punch Imlach.

The Penguins had lost consecutive games to open a best-of-seven semifinal playoff series against the hated St. Louis Blues. Before Game 3, Kelly plunked anywhere from $1,300 to $7,250—depending on which story you believe—on the dressing-room floor.

This was back when playoff money could seriously pad a player's annual salary. In the Penguins' first season, for example, Andy Bathgate was the team's highest-paid player at $25,000. Most players took summertime jobs to increase their income.

Kelly looked at his troops and said, "This is what you're playing for. Don't let the other team reach their hand in it."

The players were awed.

"I never saw that many bills," goalie Les Binkley said. "I often wondered if anybody hung behind when we went on the ice that day. It's amazing how some coaches can get teams fired up."

The Penguins stormed back to win the next two games against Scotty Bowman's Blues but ultimately lost the series, four games to two.

SON OF A SEA COOK

Hockey players are renowned for using objectionable language, a fact that made the Penguins' second coach—and later general manager—Leonard "Red" Kelly, all the more remarkable. Kelly had been around the game his entire life, but he never was heard to swear during his three-plus seasons behind Pittsburgh's bench.

This, despite owning a .423 winning percentage.

When Kelly got really mad, he'd call somebody a "Son of a Sea Cook Bottle Washer" or exclaim, "Oh, what the hang's going on out there!'"

Suffice to say, nobody had a good answer to that question during the team's franchise-record, 18-game road winless streak in 1970-71.

And you wonder if Kelly might have sworn under his breath when he walked into his office one day to find Boston Bruins coach Harry Sinden watching Penguins game film. Apparently, a Penguins office worker had given Sinden the tapes and permission to watch them in Kelly's office.

"Red went nuts," recalled sportswriter Bill Heufelder, who covered the team for the *Pittsburgh Press*. "I don't think he swore, though."

HATIN' THE BLUES

Rivalries were an important part of the NHL landscape when the Penguins joined the league in 1967. Teams played each other 10 times a season, often in home-and-home series on the weekends.

The Penguins' first fierce rival was their Western Division partner, the St. Louis Blues, who inspired venomous hatred by trotting out the hell-bent-for-leather Plager brothers—Barclay, Bill, and Bob—plus defenseman Noel Picard and a host of others.

When a Pittsburgh sportscaster asked Penguins coach Leonard "Red" Kelly prior to a playoff series if there was bad blood between the teams, he replied, "Only if it spills."

The Blues weren't comprised only of troublemakers. There was a sense of royalty about them, as well. They had some magnificent offensive players and a pair of distinguished goaltenders in Glenn Hall and Jacques Plante. A young Scotty Bowman was the coach.

"When those guys all came down the runway in St. Louis, with the organ blasting, it was tremendous," recalled Bill Heufelder, who covered the Penguins for the *Pittsburgh Press*.

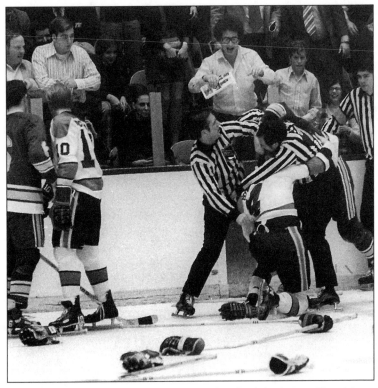

A common sight in the early days: The Penguins brawl with the St. Louis Blues. Notice how low the glass is. *(Photo courtesy of the Pittsburgh Penguins)*

The Penguins countered with the likes of feisty goalie Al Smith, wacky defenseman Bryan Watson, and scrappy hustlers such as Bryan Hextall and Glen Sather.

NHL broadcaster Mike Emrick, then a freelance writer for a Pittsburgh suburban newspaper called the *Beaver County Times*, remembered covering an Easter Sunday game in 1970 at the Civic Arena. It ended with a controversial winning goal for the Penguins and with fans pelting the Blues with garbage.

After arena workers packed the litter into garbage cans, Barclay Plager dumped it back onto the ice.

"With Bobby and Barclay, what you saw is what you got," Watson said. "They were great competitors. They were showboats and the whole bit, but that was part of it. You knew it was going to be a slugfest."

Years later, Barclay Plager had former Penguins GM Jack Riley on his radio show and said to him, "Jack, you should've paid me to come to your building. Everyone hated me!"

MAYHEM

On January 23, 1974, a record crowd of 13,324 filled the Civic Arena expecting mayhem.

They weren't disappointed.

Six days earlier, new Penguins GM Jack Button acquired notorious tough guys "Battleship" Bob Kelly and Steve Durbano from the hated St. Louis Blues. This would be their first home game in a Penguins sweater.

"I remember we were standing at center ice during warm-ups, and Durby was talking to his old teammates," recalled former Penguins center Syl Apps. "He was saying, 'How are you? How are the kids? How's your son doing?' And the first time somebody comes in front of the net, he's spearing them, saying, 'You can't be standing here!'"

Early in the second period, Durbano fought Bob Gassoff while Kelly battled Barclay Plager. The crowd was delirious by the time the buzzer sounded in a 4-1 Penguins victory. Kelly and Durbano were named co-No. 1 stars of the game, a first in team history, and they skated onto the ice with their arms raised together. The photograph depicting that moment is among the more familiar and famous in team history.

"It's funny," Apps said. "After that, the teams that used to run around all over the place against us all of a sudden weren't running around anymore."

EAR MUFF MANIA

A by-product of the Penguins' rivalry with the St. Louis Blues was intense crowd participation. Penguins fans jeered Blues defenseman Barclay Plager by chanting his first name and held up signs like the one that said, "Bucket Mouth Bowman and His Three Stooges: Barclay, Bob and Noel."

That was in reference to Blues coach Scotty Bowman and three of his hellraisers: Barclay and Bob Plager and Noel Picard.

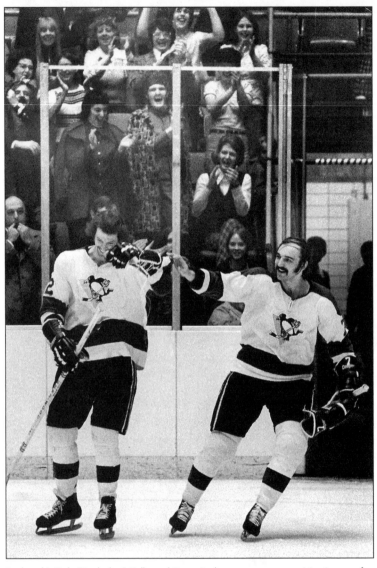

Pittsburgh's Bob "Battleship" Kelly and Steve Durbano emerge as co-No. 1 stars after a game against St. Louis in which they roughed up their former teammates.
(Photo courtesy of the Pittsburgh Penguins)

Blues fans weren't exactly wallflowers. "They used to go wild during the pregame stuff," recalled Penguins defenseman Duane Rupp.

In an effort to counteract that, and perhaps to send a message of sorts, Penguins coach Leonard "Red" Kelly made his players wear ear muffs at the start of a game January 3, 1970.

"He came in the dressing room and started passing out ear muffs, and the guys ware looking at each other like, 'Oh, man, we have to do this?'" Rupp said.

Rupp was spared the embarrassment, because he was in the starting lineup. Only players on the bench were forced to wear the ear muffs, which came in various colors.

Needless to say, it was a challenge to get through the National Anthem without laughing.

"We could barely stand on the blue line and keep a straight face," Rupp said.

The laughter died quickly. The Penguins lost, 6-0.

EMRICK ON THE SCENE

Most people know Mike Emrick as a national hockey broadcaster, or perhaps as the voice of the New Jersey Devils. Few know him as a freelance writer for a suburban Pittsburgh newspaper, but that's exactly what he was in the 1970 and '71, as he completed his studies at Geneva College in Beaver County, outside of Pittsburgh.

Emrick went to the editor of the *Beaver County Times* and said he'd cover Penguins home games for nothing if they got him a season pass.

"I was a terrible writer," Emrick said. "But I was thrilled to be there."

RAPID FIRE

For some odd reason, the Penguins have been known to score in bunches against the St. Louis Blues. The five fastest goals in team history were scored November 22, 1972, against the Blues, when Bryan Hextall, Jean Pronovost, Al McDonough, Ken Schinkel and Ron Schock all connected within 2:07 of a 10-4 victory. The final three goals marked the fastest three in team history. They came in 27 seconds.

Twenty-six years later, on December 12, 1998, Alexei Kovalev (twice), Jaromir Jagr and Stu Barnes scored the four fastest goals in team history (1:39) in a 4-3 win at St. Louis.

THE CENTURY LINE

One was a Boston Bruins reject. Another had nearly retired because of multiple knee operations, and the third couldn't break a wet paper towel with his wrist shot.

Together, they were poetry on ice.

Jean Pronovost, Lowell MacDonald, and Syl Apps, all right-handed shots, comprised the first great line in Penguins history.

Pittsburgh's Century Line, Lowell MacDonald, Jean Pronovost, and Syl Apps, celebrate Pronovost's 50th goal in 1976. *(Photo courtesy of the Pittsburgh Penguins)*

Coach Ken Schinkel put them together in January of 1974. The three combined for 107 goals that season, second in the league to Buffalo's celebrated French Connection, and Penguins publicity director Terry Schiffhauer dubbed them "The Century Line."

The trio refused to play a dump-and-chase game, preferring more of a weaving, European style.

"We used to bump into each other more than anyone else would bump us," MacDonald said.

Technically, Apps was the center, MacDonald the left winger, and Pronovost the right winger, but the positions were interchangeable.

"Lowell and I couldn't shoot the puck any more than 15 feet; that's why we did a lot of passing," said Apps, the playmaker. "Plus, Lowell couldn't see that far. I think he had a worse shot than I did, but, boy, he could pick the spot. We were a little bit of a throwback in that we didn't dump the puck and we used a lot of drop passes."

MacDonald said teammates used to kid him, saying, "Geez, one of these times the puck will actually hit the back of the net."

His reply: "It just needs to get over that line, boys."

Apps came to the Penguins in January of '71 as part of an unpopular trade that sent gritty Glen Sather (later the architect of the Edmonton Oilers' dynasty) to the New York Rangers. The deal, orchestrated by Penguins coach and GM Leonard "Red" Kelly, proved to be among the best in team history.

The Pronovost deal wasn't bad either. GM Jack Riley acquired him from Boston in 1968 in exchange for a No. 1 draft pick that turned out to be nondescript winger Frank Spring. The gimpy-kneed MacDonald came along in the 1970 intra-league draft, when Kelly talked him out of retiring.

Apps said the three players rarely spent time together off the ice. Opponents wished they'd spent less time together on it.

POLISH ARMY

Franco's Italian Army goes down in history as the best–known ethnic rooting section in Pittsburgh sports history. It was founded by second- and third-generation Italian Americans who rooted for Steelers running back Franco Harris beginning in 1972.

A few years before that, however, a group called Woytowich's Polish Army was in full bloom. Bob Woytowich was a rough-and-tumble Penguins defenseman who inspired a legion of followers.

As told in a *Pittsburgh Press* story from November 15, 1971, there were only two requirements for members of Woytowich's Polish Army: "You have to have the money to buy a general admission ticket, and you must never say a nice word about any of the Pens' opponents, collectively or individually."

PRESIDENTS DAY

Former Penguins goalie Les Binkley got knocked cold in a game one night. When the trainer came out to help him, he asked if Binkley could name the president of the United States.

"How should I know?" Binkley said. "I'm Canadian."

WILD WEEKEND

Going into the final weekend of the 1971-72 season, the Penguins couldn't have been all that optimistic about their playoff chances. They needed to tie or win at Philadelphia on Saturday, win at home against St. Louis on Sunday and hope the Buffalo Sabres won at Philadelphia.

Several minor miracles ensued.

The Penguins trailed 4-3 in the final minute at Philadelphia, but Greg Polis tied it with the goalie pulled at the 19:14 mark, tipping home Eddie Shack's low shot.

Before the next day's action, Penguins general manager Jack Riley called his colleague in Buffalo, Punch Imlach, with a word of encouragement. The irascible Imlach shot back, "You just take care of your game. We'll take care of ours."

As the Penguins were whipping the Blues, 6-2, the next night, the team made an announcement to the crowd that playoff tickets would go on sale if Buffalo was able to beat Philadelphia.

It didn't look good, because those teams went to the final minute tied 2-2. There still were eight minutes left in the Penguins' game when defenseman Dave Burrows went to the corner to retrieve a dump-in.

"As soon as I touched the puck, the building exploded with this huge cheer," Burrows said. "I thought there was a fight somewhere. I don't know if I left the puck there or turned around to look for a fight. It almost cost us, because guys were coming down on me."

Fans roared because the out-of-town scoreboard showed that Buffalo had won. The Sabres pulled it out on Gerry Meehan's desperation, 45-foot shot that sailed through the pads of Flyers goalie Doug Favell with only four seconds left (there was no overtime in those days).

"Suddenly, there was this stampede to the box office," Riley said.

Eighteen years later, the Penguins again would go to the final day of the regular season with Buffalo intimately involved in their playoff hopes. That time, however, Uwe Krupp's long slap shot in overtime at the Civic Arena gave Buffalo a 3-2 victory and sent the Penguins home for the summer.

The good news is that the Penguins got to draft fifth overall and used the selection on future superstar Jaromir Jagr.

WESTERN UNION MAN

Today, sportswriters carry laptop computers and often send their first-edition stories at the final buzzer. That wasn't the case for Bill Heufelder and his colleagues. Heufelder covered the Penguins' first several seasons for the *Pittsburgh Press*.

After every road game, he went back to his hotel, hammered out a story on his typewriter and headed to the nearest Western Union office. The story then was teletyped back to the newspaper.

In most cities, the Western Union office was within walking distance. That included Detroit, but Heufelder wasn't taking any chances after dark in that particular city.

"The office was two blocks away, but I took a cab," he said. "And the cabbie understood why."

CLEAN-UP DUTY

When Michel Briere was tearing up the Quebec Midget Leagues, another future Penguins star was watching closely. A pee-wee Pierre Larouche had clean-up duty between games.

"In between games, a few of us kids would be sweeping and cleaning," Larouche said. "We'd pick up the oranges and stuff. I remember asking [Briere] for his stick. When I watched him, I was like, 'Wow, how good is that guy?'"

THE IGLOO

Pittsburgh's hockey arena has been compared to a giant silver spaceship. Originally built to house the Civic Light Opera, it was

Pittsburgh's (Civic) Mellon Arena. *(Photo courtesy of the Pittsburgh Penguins)*

completed in 1961 at the cost of $22 million and has the largest retractable dome roof in the world (although it was never opened during a hockey game).

That's 170,000 square feet and 2,950 tons of pure Pittsburgh steel.

The other unique part of the Penguins' home rink, when the team broke into the league, was the sheet of ice. It was bigger than in most arenas. The standard NHL rink nowadays measures 200 feet long by 85 feet wide. Former Penguins winger Lowell MacDonald said the Civic Arena's sheet measured 207 x 92 until it was revamped in the mid-1970s to make way for some expensive seats.

MacDonald and his linemates, Syl Apps and Jean Pronovost, played a passing game that lent itself nicely to the big rink.

"Prony had a great set of wheels, I could skate, and Syl had a great sense of where we were and what we were doing," MacDonald said. "It was a great rink to play in when it was a bigger ice surface. We had at least one or two years there, as a line, before they took it away from us."

The fans inside the dome were pretty unique, too. Defenseman Dave Burrows grew up in Toronto, where the fans have always been knowledgeable and polite. Penguins fans were neither when the team came into existence.

"When I got there [in 1971], the fans were wild," said Burrows, whose workmanlike efforts eventually landed him in the team's Hall of Fame. "There were a lot of blue-collar workers, and they loved the physical part of it and would be so vocal about the game.

"I mean, in Toronto, people would cheer and stuff, but in Pittsburgh, people would fight in the stands. We loved it. When we started winning there for a while, I remember we had a string of sellouts, and I was just dying to get on the ice. I loved Pittsburgh and loved the people. They seemed to appreciate the style of hockey I played, I guess. They were very good for me."

HAT TRICK HISTORY

On March 24, 1971, Duane Rupp became the first Penguins defenseman to record a hat trick. He did it against the Detroit Red Wings and goaltender Jim Rutherford in an 8-2 victory at the Civic Arena.

You could imagine, then, that Rupp wasn't too pleased to see the Penguins acquire Rutherford that summer.

"I walked up to him and said, 'How the heck am I going to get any more goals now that you're on my team?'" said Rupp, who had just 21 goals in 265 games with the Penguins.

Defensemen didn't jump into the rush much in those days, so Rupp was shocked, to the say the least, with his three-goal performance.

Late in the game, with the score lopsided, coach Leonard "Red" Kelly sent Rupp onto the ice often in hopes of getting him the hat trick.

"All the guys were trying to pass it to me, telling me, 'Shoot, shoot, shoot,'" Rupp remembered. "By the time the game ended, I had to tape my arms in ice. On the third one, I had three scoops at it. I just kept shoveling, hoping it would go in. It finally did. We didn't have much to celebrate as a team that year [the Penguins won only 21 of 78 games], but that sure was fun."

SURVEY SAYS

One thing about the late Al Smith: "You never had any idea what he was going to do," said teammate Ron Schock.

Smith was the anti-establishment goalie during his two seasons with the Penguins. A real rebel.

"You could put him in a $3,000 suit, and he'd still look like he came out of an alleyway," Schock said.

On one particular road trip, Smith decided to conduct a survey on the best ways to attract women. He carried around a notebook, madly scribbling answers to questions like, "What kind of shaving cream do you use?" and "What's your opening line?" He interviewed players, stewardesses, anyone he could find.

"He did this the whole road trip," Schock recalled.

Smith's preliminary data showed that common strategies did not work and that people who wore unusual cologne or delivered weird opening lines experienced the most success.

Before he could issue a final report, however, straight-laced coach Leonard "Red" Kelly intervened. Schock remembers Kelly approaching Smith in front of the team and saying, "Smitty, that's enough with the survey. ... You'll never get a woman, anyways."

Smith went home and burned the survey in his bathtub.

LOCK 'EM IN

Fans were scarce for Pittsburgh's two fledgling sports teams in the late 1960s—the NHL's Penguins and the ABA's Pittsburgh Pipers. Both played at the Civic Arena. Tom Rooney, who later became the Penguins president, was an usher at the arena. He remembered the Pipers sometimes played immediately after an attractive high school tournament and once tried to lock fans in the building to stay and watch their game.

"It was this unbelievable thing," Rooney said. "There was a mass exodus after the high school games, and people couldn't get out. It was like, 'How in the hell do I get out of here?'"

THE NIGHT CHICAGO DIED

On October 21, 1967, the Penguins became the first expansion team to beat an established club when they doubled up the Chicago Blackhawks, 4-2, at the Civic Arena. Penguins coach George "Red" Sullivan assigned right winger Ken Schinkel—a future Penguins coach—to shadow Blackhawks star Bobby Hull. The plan worked out better than anyone had a right to expect.

Schinkel scored the second hat trick in team history and helped hold Hull without a goal.

"Kenny was a good player, a smart player," Sullivan said. "He could read Bobby pretty good."

FRENCH CONNECTION

The Buffalo Sabres had the most famous French Connection, but it was together only for part of the 1970s. The Penguins' French Connection has spanned nearly the entire history of the franchise.

It's easy to connect the dots. Start with a stately winger named Jean Pronovost, who hailed from Shawinigan Falls, Quebec. He became the first Penguin to score 30 goals, in 1971-72, and the first to score 50, in 1975-76.

"He was an underrated, dedicated player who rarely had an off game," recalled former linemate Syl Apps.

During Pronovost's rookie year, a small-framed centerman named Michel Briere was racking up 161 points in 50 games for the Shawinigan Bruins of the Quebec Major Junior Hockey League. That summer, the Penguins drafted 5-foot-10, 160-pound Briere 26th overall and watched him blossom into an impact player in his rookie year. His life tragically was cut short by a car accident shortly after that season.

Briere had also played a bit of junior hockey for the Sorel Blackhawks of the QMJHL. Five years later, a flashy young Sorel forward named Pierre Larouche set a Canadian junior hockey record by logging 251 points in 67 games. Larouche's brother, Maurice, had played junior with Briere.

The Penguins took Pierre Larouche eighth overall. He scored 31 goals as a rookie and 50 in his second year, becoming, at 20, the youngest NHL player ever to score 50 goals.

In 1977, Larouche was traded to Montreal, the birthplace of a kid named Mario Lemieux, who in 1983-84 smashed Larouche's single-season junior points record (although Larouche's record of 157 assists stayed intact). Lemieux piled up 282 points in 70 games with Laval of the QMJHL. He would become one of the greatest players in NHL history and would be the team owner when the Penguins drafted yet another ballyhooed QMJHL product, goaltender Marc-Andre Fleury, first overall in 2003.

Fleury made the Penguins roster as an 18-year-old and stopped 46 of 48 shots in his NHL debut. For a short time at the start of his career, he lived with Lemieux's family.

Oh, and Fleury was born in Sorel, where Briere and Larouche played junior hockey.

GONE FISHIN'

It might just be an old fish story, but former Penguins equipment manager John Doolan swears it's true.

The team returned to the Civic Arena at about 3 a.m. after a bus trip to Buffalo—no word on whether alcohol was served—when to their delight they discovered an outdoorsman show set up for the next day. It included a pool of trout, where kids could fish for prizes.

Players such as goalie Les Binkley and center Bryan Hextall suddenly rediscovered their inner children.

"The guys saw all these trout, grabbed a big net from one of the booths and started scooping," Doolan said. "One guy went right in the pool, about two feet deep.

"People from the show came in the next day and wondered where all the trout were."

2

ON THE BRINK

(1975-1983)

JOHN DENVER'S FAULT?

No team, not even the Philadelphia Flyers, has tortured the Penguins more than the New York Islanders, who administered three devastating playoff blows between 1975 and 1993.

One nearly proved fatal to Pittsburgh's eight-year-old NHL franchise.

It occurred in the spring of 1975, as the Penguins became the second team in league history to blow a three-games-to-none lead in a best-of-seven series.

Many of the players who participated cite a delay between Games 3 and 4 at Nassau Coliseum as the turning point.

Game 4 should have been played on a one-day rest, but a John Denver concert fouled things up. The game was moved to two days after the concert—to Sunday, April 20—so it could be televised nationally.

Somewhere in there, the Penguins lost their edge. Or so some say.

"I never quite forgave John Denver," said former Penguins captain Ron Schock. "I think the momentum turned with that concert."

Teammate Syl Apps wished the Penguins had flown back to Pittsburgh between Games 3 and 4. But the team was hemorrhaging money.

"Back then, you'd say, 'What's it going to cost us to go home?'"Apps said. "Today, they would have flown out right after that third game."

One former Penguin, Pierre Larouche, strongly disagrees with the notion that the delay caused a shift in momentum. He said it simply was a matter of overconfidence.

"After the third game, management threw a party for us," recalled Larouche, then a rookie. "And everybody thought it was over. It was not. You can't use the delay as an excuse. We got whacked."

CARD SHARK

One night, former Penguins general manager Baz Bastien took out his glass right eye and put it on the table during a card game. Another player looked at him and said, "Baz, quit looking at the cards."

TRASH MAN

Hockey players are a superstitious sort, sometimes to the point of psychosis. Take goaltender Nick Ricci, for example. He couldn't walk past a trash can before going onto the ice.

His reasoning?

"If you walk by trash, you'll play like garbage."

When Ricci first was recalled from the minors in 1979, he asked equipment man John Doolan to move all the trash cans.

After a while, however, it became clear that all the superstition in the world wasn't going to help Ricci.

"He wasn't doing anything," Doolan recalled, "so I finally said, 'Hey, enough of this,' and moved the trash cans back to where they were."

SHEDDEN'S GRANDMOTHER

There wasn't much to laugh about during the Penguins' 8-2 loss at Toronto on January 24, 1983.

Well, not until Doug Shedden's grandmother made her way to the team bench.

Shedden had grown up near Toronto, so several family members were in attendance, including his grandmother. There was an exit at Maple Leaf Gardens where fans could walk right past the visiting team's bench, and, sure enough, an elderly woman came down to comfort her grandson ... with about eight minutes left in the game ... and the puck in play.

"She gave me a big hug and kiss and said, 'Don't you worry about it, there'll be better days,'" Shedden remembered. "I said, 'Nanny, Nanny, it's OK. Go back and sit in your seat.'"

Coach Eddie Johnston was dumbfounded. Shedden's teammates were folded over in laughter.

"There were about nine guys who had to put their heads under the boards," he said, "because their faces were turning purple."

MISTAKEN IDENTITY?

Legend has it that then-general manager Baz Bastien, on October 18, 1978, sent a first-round draft pick to the Montreal Canadiens believing that the player he acquired—Rod Schutt—actually was future Hall of Famer Steve Shutt.

Rod Schutt insists it's a fable.

"That was actually a locker-room joke," Schutt said. "Guys would say, '[Bastien] only has one eye, so he only saw the last name.' It wasn't true, because he knew quite well who he was getting. Pittsburgh was going to draft me originally, and we had conversations before the draft."

Schutt laughed and added, "Every once in a while he used to call me Steve."

CHICO WAS THE MAN

New York Islanders coach Al Arbour made a critical move after his team lost the first three games of a 1975 playoff series against the Penguins. He replaced goalie Billy Smith with Glenn "Chico" Resch.

Resch responded with four consecutive victories in which he allowed four total goals.

He later joked that the critical point in the series occurred in Game 6, when he kissed the goal post.

"It had been so sweet to me," he said. "They must have hit six or seven."

Resch remembered his luck continuing into Game 7, when the Penguins' vaunted Century Line—Syl Apps, Jean Pronovost and Lowell MacDonald—swarmed the Islanders' goal early at the Civic Arena.

"In the first few minutes, someone came down the slot and hit me in the mask," Resch said. "The puck went into the corner, came right into the slot again and, bang, right off the goal post. That's when I thought, 'Hey, you know what? This may last one more game.'"

Resch's playoff goals-against average against the Penguins—1.00 in four games—stands as the best mark for any opposing goaltender, just ahead of Hall of Famer Jacques Plante (1.33 in three games).

HIS TEETH FELL OUT

The poor girl who told Jimmy Roberts his room at the Forum Inn wasn't ready probably still remembers his reaction.

As broadcaster Mike Lange remembers it, Roberts, an assistant coach for the Penguins in the mid-1980s, was tired and cranky after a full day of travel. A lot of the guys were, because the team had just traversed the country. They were playing the Los Angeles Kings the next night at the Great Western Forum.

When the young hotel desk worker told Roberts none of the rooms was ready—that, in fact, there were no reservations for the Pittsburgh Penguins—he lost it.

"You have to know Jimmy," Lange said. "He was part of the old guard, played for the Canadiens in the '70s and believed in playing hard and working hard at your job.

"He said, 'This is the *Pittsburgh Penguins*, we're staying here, 25 rooms, we're spending a lot of money here.' She said, 'I don't have the keys, I don't have the rooms, but if you can wait, we'll clean the rooms.'

"Jimmy slams his hand on the counter again, and when he hit it, his bridge came out of his mouth, flew in the air and came down on the counter. This girl was 20 at most. Her eyes got big as a frisbee. Well, in the same motion, Jimmy picked up his teeth with his left hand—didn't miss a beat—and kept yelling."

Word traveled quickly. A brutal day suddenly became bearable.

"One of the funniest moments I've experienced," Lange said.

SPINNER SPENCER

Brian "Spinner" Spencer played only 86 games for the Penguins, from 1977 to 1979, but no one who shared the smallest part of that time with him will ever forget.

"He was unique," recalled teammate Greg Malone, whose family housed Spencer for a time. "If you got to know him, he'd give you the shirt off his back."

Brian "Spinner" Spencer made the dressing room a lively place.
(Photo courtesy of the Pittsburgh Penguins)

Former Penguins winger Lowell MacDonald remembered a vintage Spinner moment from a slow afternoon in Los Angeles, when the Penguins arrived early for practice.

Three players decided to wage a contest to see who could chew the most pieces of gum. One finally gagged and spit his wad into a garbage can. The curly-haired Spencer, who'd been watching silently, walked to the trash can, fished it out and stuffed it in his mouth.

He added a few fresh pieces and won the contest.

"That was Spinner at his best," MacDonald said. "He sat there watching this thing, and then he figured out a way to win with a whole lot less effort. He had a lot of guys rolling on the floor."

The bad times, however, far outweighed the good in Spencer's life. Both he and his father were shot to death in separate incidents, 18 years apart.

His father, Roy Spencer, was killed in a shootout with Royal Canadian Mounted police after holding a Canadian Broadcasting Company television station in Prince George, British Columbia, at gunpoint. He was incensed because the station did not carry his son's NHL debut with the Toronto Maple Leafs that night after it had announced it would.

Eighteen years later, Brian Spencer was shot to death in a friend's pick-up truck in Florida. He had reportedly been involved with several shady characters.

Those who knew Spencer well said he had a big heart and lots of quirks.

"He could draw pictures like you wouldn't believe," Malone said. "He was also chiseled, with big, strong fingers and toes. He used to jump on a table and land on it with his toes curled, then jump back down and land on his toes."

NOT SO SILENT NIGHT

A 5-3 loss at Minnesota on December 23, 1978, could not dampen the Penguins' spirits. The team was winning regularly, and it was headed home for the holidays.

Maybe that explains why hulking forward Peter Mahovlich was compelled to orchestrate a round of Christmas carols.

"There he was, with sheet music, leading the carols," recalled goaltender Greg Millen. "I'll never forget it as long as I live—a six-foot-five guy on a Continental Airlines commercial flight singing away. It was incredible. Everybody sang."

'WE HAVE A PROBLEM'

Former Penguins trainer Kenny Carson figured it would be a nice gesture to lend the Penguins' equipment truck to winger Lowell MacDonald in the summer of 1975, as long as MacDonald brought it back before training camp.

MacDonald had a lot of things to move from Pittsburgh to his new summer home in Nova Scotia, so he accepted Carson's offer and drove his family in the large truck adorned with Penguins logos.

A month later, MacDonald got a phone call. It was Carson.

"He says, 'We have a problem. The team has gone bankrupt, and they tell me we need to have all the assets here,'" MacDonald said. "I said, 'Kenny, I am not driving the truck 1,280 miles back to Pittsburgh. You have to be kidding. If they want it bad enough, they can either come get it or call the Mounties.'"

NEW LOWS

The 1983-84 Penguins generally are regarded as the worst team in franchise history. A team-record 48 players were used, and the club finished with a franchise-worst 38 points.

The season-ticket base was 2,170 in the 16,033-seat arena, and the team lost $5 million. People were sure the Penguins were going to move. Some of the fans who bothered to show up did so with bags on their heads.

"You had so few fans that the boo birds would really stick out," remembered winger Bob Errey, then a rookie. "I remember coming down the runway and hearing the chants—'Errey sucks!'—or something like that. I couldn't give away tickets back then. The one promising thing was that if we did get last place, we'd be able to pick up this French-Canadian kid named Mario Lemieux."

ONE-MAN CLUB

When Eddie Johnston joined the Penguins organization as coach in 1980, the team did not have a farm club. It wouldn't own one until 1999, but at least it had affiliations. Johnston didn't even have that his first year.

"We had 23 guys, total, at training camp," he said. "And [left winger] Jim Hamilton was our farm club."

TWIST OF FATE

The man largely responsible for the New York Islanders' dynasty—and thus for much Penguins' misery—once worked inside the walls of the Civic Arena.

In fact, he was there when the place opened.

Bill Torrey, later the Islanders' general manager, was the marketing man for Pittsburgh's American Hockey League team, the Hornets, in the early 1960s. He worked for legendary promoter John H. Harris, who founded the Ice Capades, which used to open each year in Pittsburgh.

And in 1961, Torrey stood on the floor of the brand new Civic Arena with former Pittsburgh Mayor Joseph Barr.

Torrey kept an office at the arena until 1968 and continued to promote events in the building even after he had moved on to work for Charlie Finley with the Oakland Seals, one of a group of six expansion teams, including the Penguins, that joined the NHL in 1967.

Torrey's scouting staff with the Islanders included former Penguins player Earl Ingarfield and uncovered many talented players.

In later years, the Torrey-built Islanders dethroned the two-time Stanley Cup Champion Penguins in the second round of the 1993 playoffs, and to add one last touch of misery, Torrey was president of the Florida Panthers team that defeated the Penguins in the Eastern Conference finals in 1996.

LOUD AND CLEAR

Late Penguins general manager Baz Bastien was known to fly off the handle now and again, which is why defenseman Ron Stackhouse made it a point to stuff cotton balls in his ears whenever Bastien addressed the team.

Stackhouse would nod his head in the affirmative, as if he were listening, then remove the cotton when Bastien left.

Rookie centerman Mark Johnson probably wished he had some cotton after what Bastien said to him in 1981, following the Penguins' decisive, double-overtime playoff loss to the St. Louis Blues.

Johnson had missed a golden chance in each overtime, hitting three posts on two chances. "Kid, you coulda' been a hero tonight," Bastien said, "but you blew it."

HISTORY ALTERED

Nobody knows for sure exactly what turned the Penguins' playoff series against the New York Islanders in 1975. All that's certain is that the Penguins squandered a three-games-to-none lead—and that both franchises never were the same.

The Penguins sank into bankruptcy that summer. The Islanders moved toward a dynasty that would result in four consecutive Stanley Cups (1980-83).

"I always wondered if we'd won—and we're talking winning one more game—what would we have gone on to?" former Penguins defenseman Dave Burrows said. "You look at the Islanders, they went on to become a dynasty. That gave them the confidence to be a Stanley Cup team."

"We made the Islanders," added former Penguins winger Lowell MacDonald. "Their attendance was not good, but once they turned it around, they picked it up and were never the same after that. I still believe their guys should have sent us thank-you cards. That franchise was in bad shape. We weren't anywhere near the condition they were in."

That's debatable, considering the Penguins were $6.5 million in debt and soon to be bankrupt. If they'd won that series, they would have earned enough revenues in the next round to avert bankruptcy.

Then again, if they'd won that series, they might not have sunk to the point they did in the early 1980s—and Mario Lemieux might never have worn a Penguins sweater.

Along that line of thinking, the 1975 Penguins actually did the franchise a favor.

Right?

"Damn right we did," Syl Apps said.

STAN GILBERTSON

Sometimes, there is humor in tragedy. Such a time occurred at Penguins training camp in 1978, when left winger Stan Gilbertson stood on a scale at the Civic Arena, not long after losing his leg in a jeep accident.

Head coach Johnny Wilson had been pestering Gilbertson about his weight before the accident. When Gilbertson was released from the hospital, he went to the arena, stepped on a scale and started yelling, "Johnny! Johnny!"

Wilson thought Gilbertson had fallen or dropped his crutches. When he ran into the room, Gilbertson looked at him and said, "I made weight, Johnny, I made weight!"

TAKE THIS JOB ...

Talk about ending a career in style. Lou Morrison, a nondescript right winger who played for the Penguins from 1974-78, decided he'd had enough as he and a few teammates drove to his summer home on the Jersey shore.

Morrison stopped his car at the top of a bridge, opened the trunk and threw his equipment bag into the ocean.

"He said, 'I'll never play another hockey game,'" equipment manager John Doolan recalled. "At an alumni game the next year, he said he needed equipment, and I said, 'Oh yeah? Get a fishing line.'"

One of Morrison's former teammates, defenseman Tom Edur, retired at age 23 and became a Jehovah's Witness.

NEVER AGAIN

No coach has started and finished four consecutive seasons behind the Penguins' bench. That includes Eddie Johnston, who had two cracks at the job.

But Johnston owns a longevity streak of another sort that remains an NHL record. He was the most recent goalie to play every minute of every game in a single season.

A torn ear lobe, three broken noses, and 70 stitches failed to keep Johnston from missing a second of the 1963-64 season with the Boston Bruins.

"That's something that will stand forever," said former Penguins goaltender Ron Tugnutt.

Remembered Johnston: "The trainer was the back-up goalie. That was for all teams. You only had one goalie then."

Johnston, who played without a mask, finished the season with a record of 18-40-12—that's 70 games—with a 3.01 goals-against average. The closest he came to missing any action was when a slap shot tore his left earlobe. He got it stitched and returned to the crease.

He wasn't so lucky at other times in his career. When he got hurt badly enough to leave a game, a back-up goalie—if it wasn't the trainer—had to be pulled from the crowd. One time it was a fireman.

Pens coach Eddie Johnston gives an earful to a linesman.
(Photo courtesy of the Pittsburgh Penguins)

"It was a fire chief in Boston, and I had to hold his leg down it was shaking so bad," Johnston said. "He was nervous."

BROKEN GLASS

All the losing in the mid-1980s was enough to make a guy want to eat glass.

Literally.

Paul Steigerwald, the Penguins' radio play-by-play man, remembers going on TV in 1984 and saying that defenseman Bryan Maxwell was struggling because of a knee injury.

This did not please Maxwell, who took great exception to the term "struggling." He confronted Steigerwald, who recounted their brief but memorable interaction.

"He took a wine glass, bit it, chewed it up into a million pieces and spit into the palm of my hand."

PROFOUND MESSAGE

New York Islanders coach Al Arbour delivered a basic but powerful message to his sagging players before Game 4 of their 1975 series against the Penguins. The Islanders had lost the first three games.

"He said, 'If there's one guy who doesn't think we can win the next game and this series, I want you to take your stuff off and go to the dressing room right now,'" recalled ex-Islanders forward Eddie Westfall. "That was profound."

And it worked. The Islanders came back to win four consecutive games. Westfall scored the game-winner in a 1-0, Game 7 victory.

"It's not about winning the next game, it's about winning the next shift," Westfall said. "It really simplifies it. I remember that idea resonating from practice the day before the fourth game right to the last shift of the seventh game, and that's all we thought about—taking it a shift at a time. It was almost to the point of sickening. When you think about it, it's so repetitious.

"I was always worried we would have too many men on the ice, because guys were just dying to jump over the boards. We almost had to sedate guys between periods."

When the series ended, the Penguins were the ones who needed medication.

BANKRUPT

The Penguins are the only franchise in National Hockey League history that could answer, "Which time?," if somebody asked when they had gone bankrupt.

The first time occurred in 1975, although technically the franchise did not declare bankruptcy but was placed in "receivership" with a debt of $6.5 million.

No one who worked at the Civic Arena will forget the sight of Penguins employees scrambling to recover their belongings before the IRS padlocked the doors to the Penguins' offices.

The IRS had slapped the Penguins with a $532,000 lien for failure to pay withholding taxes.

"They came in and took files and everything else," said Elaine Heufelder, who worked at the arena and would later work for the Penguins. "It was a mad scramble. It was funny but not funny, if you know what I mean."

Yes, the players knew exactly what that meant. That season had been a constant exercise in cutting corners.

"There were things that went on, with nickeling and diming everyone," defenseman Dave Burrows recalled. "You only got one towel in the dressing room, and we used to have oranges in the dressing room, and then they cut those out, and you'd think, 'Geez, we're in awful shape.'

"We were all worried. As a player, you don't want to go through a summer thinking, 'What are you going to do with your house?'"

"Conditions were not ideal," added former centerman Syl Apps. "If you had a dozen sticks, you'd be lucky. I remember a couple times, guys only had one pair of skates. If you broke a blade, too bad."

A year later, the Penguins hired a general manager who was used to working in such conditions. They brought in Baz Bastien, who'd been the assistant general manager for the bankrupt Kansas City Scouts.

BENCH-CLEARING BRAWL

The night before the Pittsburgh Steelers played in their last Super Bowl under coach Chuck Noll, the Penguins went bonkers at the Civic Arena, setting a franchise penalty-minute record with a lot of help from the Edmonton Oilers.

The trouble began when defenseman Kim Clackson drilled 18-year-old Oilers phenom Wayne Gretzky after Gretzky missed a scoring chance. Oilers tough guy Dave Semenko took great exception.

Order wasn't restored for more than an hour.

The Oilers were the first to leave their bench, a fact that prompted Penguins captain Orest Kindrachuk to wave to his bench for reinforcements. Clackson and Semenko fought three times, including once with Clackson in the penalty box.

Oilers coach Glen Sather threw a water bottle and reportedly tried to climb the glass to get at a heckler.

"Clackson deliberately tried to injure Gretzky with his stick," Sather told reporters after the game. "A goof like that shouldn't be in the league. That stuff went out with the dark ages."

Each team had four players ejected, and the game took nearly three hours. The last fight of the night saw the Oilers' Colin Campbell—the NHL's future Lord of Discipline—square off with Greg Malone with 2:45 remaining.

Colin Campbell, the NHL's future czar of discipline, was a scrapper with the Penguins. *(Photo courtesy of the Pittsburgh Penguins)*

The Penguins were assessed 144 penalty minutes. The teams combined for 247. Penguins defenseman Russ Anderson set a team mark with 51 penalty minutes himself.

The next day, Anderson and his wife modeled the team's new black-and-gold jerseys at a team function on scenic Mt. Washington. And the Steelers beat the Los Angeles Rams, 31-19.

FOUR-GOAL NIGHT

For a 15-year stretch beginning in 1974, trips to Philadelphia were like trips to the dentist for the Penguins. It wasn't always a treat when the Flyers visited the Civic Arena, either.

On one such visit—December 13, 1980—Paul Gardner became the first player in Penguins history to score four goals in a game. To no avail. Flyers star Bobby Clarke countered with a hat trick in a 6-5 victory.

Still, it was a night to remember for Gardner, who excitedly ambled up to the wives' room shortly after the final buzzer.

"Even the wives gave me a standing ovation," he said.

Gardner was the ultimate garbage man in front of the net.

"We used to joke that you had to get it by him and the goaltender to score a goal," teammate Randy Carlyle said.

LUCKY PIERRE

During the 1975-76 season, at age 20, Penguins forward Pierre Larouche became the youngest player in NHL history to score 50 goals.

"Lucky" Pierre, as he was called, also became one of the only players, presumably, to be put in a kissing booth at a shopping mall. It happened in the summer of 1976, when he and teammate Wayne Bianchin were asked to staff the booth for charity.

Each kiss was worth $1 to Children's Hospital.

"Oh my God, I felt like Elvis Presley that day," Larouche remembered. "I went to the mall with all those cops around me and all those people. It was pretty wild. I didn't want to go."

Well, it wasn't a bad thing once the kissing started, was it?

"All depends," Larouche said. "And if my mom would've seen me, she would've died."

Around the same time, popular Pittsburgh sportscaster Myron Cope hosted a contest called "Win A Date With Pierre." More than 15,000 letters poured in, each woman stating in 20 words why she would like to go out with Larouche.

One letter stood out.

"It was a Philly girl, the niece of [Flyers goalie] Bernie Parent, and she said if she didn't win, she'd have the Broad Street Bullies kick the hell out of me," Larouche said. "I saw it and said, 'You don't have to worry about that; they're already doing it.'"

HE'S FALLEN AND HE CAN'T GET UP

Goalie Greg Millen was sure he was headed back to the minors in 1979 when general manager Baz Bastien called him into his office after an 8-3 loss at the Olympia in Detroit.

Bastien had been a professional goalie himself, one whose career ended at age 29 when he lost his right eye in practice after getting hit with a shot.

"He pulled me in the office and went to put his hand on a chair—very firmly—and said, 'Kid, this is your short side,'" Millen recalled.

"Well, he grabbed the swivel chair, and the swivel chair was on plastic, and it slipped. He fell down behind the desk. To this day, I'm sure he would've sent me down if he didn't fall.

"Instead, he just looked at me and said, 'Get the hell out of here!'"

LOOK MA, NO HAIR

Paul Gardner had just been acquired from the Toronto Maple Leafs in November of 1980. He was nervous as he walked late into the Penguins dressing room to meet his new teammates. One of them was left winger Ross Lonsberry.

What Gardner saw next nearly made him run for his life.

"[Lonsberry] sat down and took off his toupee," Gardner said. "It caught me by surprise because I'd played against him and never knew."

Lonsberry kept the toupee on the top shelf of his locker stall. One time, at gate 3 at the old Chicago Stadium, he pushed the door open on a typically windy winter's night, and the toupee blew off his head.

"He had to run and chase it down," broadcaster Mike Lange said.

Lonsberry removed the toupee for games and practices, leaving nothing but a bald head under his helmet. Gardner doubts Lonsberry would admit it, but he wore a buckle on his helmet, while everyone else used a clip.

STRANGE COMPANY

Guess who Islanders forward Eddie Westfall drank with the night he eliminated the Penguins from the 1975 playoffs?

The Penguins, that's who.

Westfall could barely think straight after scoring the only goal in Game 7 of an exhilarating but exhausting series that saw the Islanders erase a three-games-to-none deficit and win the final game in Pittsburgh.

"I just remember sitting there, reflecting on the series," Westfall said. "By the time I looked up, everybody was gone except the trainers. When I got dressed and went outside the locker room, I couldn't find any of my teammates."

Westfall encountered center Syl Apps and some other Penguins in an arena corridor. Apps wondered why Westfall was all by himself.

"I told him, 'Everybody left. Where are you guys going?'" Westfall said. "He said, 'The Pleasure Bar.' So I went with the Penguins players and their wives to the Pleasure Bar and sat there drinking until sunrise."

Westfall and Apps had plenty to talk about: Apps' father, Syl Sr., played for Toronto in 1942, when the Maple Leafs became the first team in NHL history—and the only team besides the Islanders—to rally from a three-games-to-none deficit to win a playoff series.

BALTIMORE EXPRESS

The 1983-84 Penguins were among the worst teams in NHL history, but their minor-league affiliate, the Baltimore Skipjacks, were pretty darn good.

Some would say that is because players who should have been in Pittsburgh were dispatched to Baltimore. The Penguins, after all, were in the hunt for the top overall draft pick, which everybody knew was going to be Mario Lemieux.

"Around Christmastime, they just started to ship everybody out, and the story became that they were moving us down so they could get the No. 1 pick, and it was hard to live with that," recalled winger Paul Gardner. "But we made the best of it in Baltimore."

In fact, the Skipjacks won 16 games in a row that season, setting an American Hockey League record. The Penguins won only 16 games all season.

Phil Bourque, a future member of the Penguins' Stanley Cup teams, said that before each game during the streak, the Skipjacks would take the jersey of the player whose number corresponded to the win total and hang it up in the dressing room.

Before win No. 13, for example, the team hung Jim Hamilton's jersey in the room, and everybody touched it before the game.

"We always used to joke that we'd love to play an exhibition game against the Penguins," Bourque said.

The Skipjacks swept their first-round playoff series behind former Penguins starting goalie Roberto Romano. They won it so quickly, however, that they had to wait 15 days to play in the second round and were quickly dispatched. Their coach was Gene Ubriaco, who would later coach the Penguins.

BLACK AND GOLD

Much to the chagrin of the Boston Bruins, the Penguins wore black and gold uniforms for the first time on January 30, 1980, in a 4-3 loss to the St. Louis Blues.

The Penguins were looking to capitalize on Pittsburgh's new "City of Champions" status and attract more fan support by switching from their familiar blue and white. The Super-Bowl champion Pittsburgh Steelers and the World Series-champion Pittsburgh Pirates both wore black and gold.

So did the Bruins, who lodged a protest with the league. The Penguins prevailed by arguing that a black and gold precedent had been set by the Pittsburgh Pirates NHL hockey club in the early 1920s.

LETHAL POWER PLAY

Hard to believe, but true: The Penguins' most successful power play did not have Mario Lemieux on it. Or Jaromir Jagr or Paul Coffey or Ron Francis.

No, the team-record success rate of 24.5 percent was set in 1981-82, when the Penguins scored 99 power-play goals in 404 attempts.

A big key to their success was the use of basketball-style picks. Eddie Johnston was the first NHL coach to employ such picks on the power play. He got his ideas from Boston Celtics coach Tom Heinsohn when the two were working in Beantown.

"E.J. had three pick plays," defenseman Randy Carlyle recalled. "We'd do one off a faceoff, where you'd put the puck to an area and somebody would be freed on a pick and go get it. All teams played the same basic box then. We'd also pick a guy up near the point, then sneak a guy behind him. It was wide open."

Carlyle, coming off a Norris Trophy-winning season, was the quarterback. Right winger Rick Kehoe was the sniper. He'd catch goalies moving off the post and flick pucks into the upper corners. Center Paul Gardner took a beating in front but got his stick on everything. Tough guy Pat Boutette was known to use his stick on opposing players, and he also ran effective picks down low. Rookie Mike Bullard was a sharpshooter in reserve.

TRAGEDY STRIKES

On March 15, 1983, Penguins general manager Baz Bastien died in a car accident on his way home from a dinner sponsored by the Professional Hockey Writers Association.

The Associated Press account of the accident went like this:

Randy Carlyle quarterbacked the Penguins' most successful power play and was the only defenseman in team history to win the Norris Trophy.
(Photo by Paul Salva, courtesy of the Pittsburgh Penguins)

"Penguins general manager Allege 'Baz' Bastien, his driving impaired by alcohol and the loss of one eye, died after his car rammed a motorcycle, authorities say."

Earlier in the evening, marketing director Paul Steigerwald spent time with Bastien, a colorful, cigar-chomping, old-time hockey guy who often paced the Civic Arena halls at break-neck speed.

"It was about 5 p.m., and he was puffing on a cigar and sipping on a cocktail he had poured from a bottle he kept in a cabinet behind his desk," Steigerwald said. "Baz was in a reflective mood that day, so I started asking him questions about the loss of his eye (during a practice when he played goalie decades earlier), his previous heart bypass surgery and other personal matters."

Bastien, one of the true characters of the game, had been the coach of the Pittsburgh Hornets' Calder-Cup winning AHL team in 1967. He went on to have the second longest tenure (527 games) of any

Colorful GM Baz Bastien died in a tragic car accident. *(Photo courtesy of the Pittsburgh Penguins)*

Penguins GM except Craig Patrick but had a winning percentage of just .447.

One of the highlights of Bastien's career came on June 13, 1978, when he acquired defenseman Randy Carlyle and winger George Ferguson in exchange for defenseman Dave Burrows.

Ferguson won a playoff series against Buffalo with an overtime goal in 1979, and Carlyle won the Norris Trophy as the league's best defenseman two years later.

THE INCREDIBLE HULK

The late Brian "Spinner" Spencer earned his nickname for his whirling-dervish style of play. Off the ice, he put his manic energy into building a mind-boggling vehicle he called, "The Incredible Hulk."

It was a $35,000, diesel-powered vehicle that took four years to build. It had the body of a Dodge van sitting atop a 2.5 ton U.S. Army surplus truck skeleton.

And that wasn't all.

"His whole dash was covered with all kinds of instruments he took from an airplane," recalled teammate Greg Malone. "If he went over a pothole, he could tell you how deep it was and all this stuff because of the instruments he had."

The Penguins released Spencer in 1979, a day after he said to eminent broadcaster Bob Prince during a televised interview, "I don't want to be associated with a bird that can't fly."

SUPERSTAR

Pierre Larouche was the first flamboyant star in Penguins history. The buzz began when GM Jack Button drafted Larouche eighth overall in 1974.

Larouche had scored 94 goals and a league-record 251 points the year before in the Quebec Major Junior Hockey League. He notched a hat trick in his first training camp scrimmage and wound up with 33 goals in his rookie season.

He also rankled a few teammates with his cocky demeanor.

"We all came from the old school, and he was kind of in the new generation," winger Lowell MacDonald said. "But he came in with unbelievable hype, and he lived up to it."

Equipment man John Doolan saw as much when he rejoined the Penguins in 1976.

"Before my first game back, Pierre skated by me and said, 'Kid, I'll show you what they pay me to do here,'" Doolan said.

Popular Pittsburgh sportscaster Myron Cope announces the winner of the "Win a Date with Pierre" contest as Pierre Larouche listens. *(Photo courtesy of the Pittsburgh Penguins)*

On the second-period faceoff, Larouche raked the puck from Philadelphia's Bobby Clarke, skated through the Flyers and deked goalie Bernie Parent for a spectacular goal.

CONTROVERSIAL CALL

Philadelphia wasn't always such a horrible place for the Penguins. They had, after all, clinched their first playoff berth with a victory at the Spectrum in 1970.

Four years later, however, they embarked on a 15-year winless streak in the City of Brotherly Shove, where the Flyers intimidated everyone.

That included the referees, the Penguins maintained, after a historic 1-1 tie on December 20, 1979. The tie gave the Flyers a 27-game unbeaten streak, tied for longest in NHL history. They would stretch the streak to 35 games, longest in pro sports history.

The Penguins believe that only a few bad decisions by referee Dave Newell allowed it to happen.

Pittsburgh led, 1-0, when Newell whistled defenseman Bob Stewart for hooking with 4:39 left.

"A horrible call," goalie Greg Millen later opined.

Philadelphia defenseman Behn Wilson tied it with a power-play goal off his foot. The Penguins argued vehemently that the goal should have been disallowed because of a kick. Penguins color analyst Terry Schiffhauer said over the air that Newell was "gutless."

But it was the Penguins who felt as if their guts had been ripped out. Just another miserable night at the Spectrum, where they would lose on each of their next 23 visits.

CRITICAL DECISION

The Penguins have been rumored to be leaving Pittsburgh, or folding altogether, countless times since the inception of the franchise in 1967.

It almost happened for real in the summer of 1983, just a year before the team drafted its savior, Mario Lemieux.

At the time, the DeBartolo family of Youngstown, Ohio, owned both of the professional teams that played at the Civic Arena—the Penguins and the Pittsburgh Spirit soccer team.

The Spirit had been attracting 10,000 fans per game for a full year—outdrawing the Penguins—but both teams were losing money.

Former Penguins marketer Tom Rooney recalled a DeBartolo family meeting in Youngstown that summer.

"There really seemed to be a sense that they should bail out of one or the other," Rooney recalled. "They decided to keep both teams, but if it came down to one or the other, they would have gotten rid of the Penguins. There was no hope at the time. Mario wasn't on the radar yet."

Actually, GM Eddie Johnston was well aware of Lemieux, as were other teams. The Montreal Canadiens, for example, had traded former Penguin Pierre Larouche to the Hartford Whalers in 1981 for Hartford's first pick in 1983, praying it would be the first pick overall.

Former Penguins president Paul Martha recalled there being "some question" about keeping the Penguins but said the DeBartolos kept the franchise because they had control of the arena and certain revenue streams.

The Penguins never were a money-making venture for Edward DeBartolo Sr., who oversaw the San Francisco 49ers' Super Bowl-winning teams. But his stable ownership helped lead the Penguins to their glory days.

"A lot of people felt that the DeBartolos, because they were in Youngstown, didn't have that much to do with or care about the Penguins," Martha said. "That was very much untrue. I talked daily with Mr. DeBartolo. When we had a bad game, I would hear about it very early in the morning the next day."

NO ICE?

When the Penguins showed up in Johnstown, Pennsylvania, for training camp in 1982, they were greeted with a slight problem.

No ice.

A combination of warm weather and machine malfunction at the Johnstown War Memorial Arena—site of filming for the movie *Slapshot*—put camp plans on hold.

"Half the guys headed back to Pittsburgh, and half the guys headed to the golf course," recalled center Greg Malone. "Practices were canceled for two days."

Said winger Paul Gardner: "It was pretty comical. It was also beautiful outside, so we just kind of walked the streets for a few days. That was different."

ONE GOAL: MARIO

Eddie Johnston will deny the accusation, but it seemed rather obvious that he, shall we say, "created conditions" by which his team found it difficult to win during the 1983-84 season.

Johnston, then the Penguins' general manager, knew that by finishing last overall, the Penguins would be guaranteed a chance to take Mario Lemieux, the sort of player, Johnston said, who "comes along once in a lifetime. Maybe."

It's not as if Johnston had to work overtime to make sure his '83-84 team stunk. It wasn't exactly rife with overachievers. But he helped push it over the edge by doing things like sending goaltender Roberto Romano to the minors late in the season when Romano was playing well.

In his place, Johnston brought up a goalie by the name of Vincent Tremblay, who allowed 24 goals in four games … his only games in a Penguins sweater and last of his NHL career.

In early March, Johnston traded defenseman Randy Carlyle, three years removed from winning the Norris Trophy as the league's best defenseman, to the Winnipeg Jets for a player to be named later.

Much later. Moe Mantha arrived after the season.

Carlyle had been injured, but on the morning of the trade, he told Penguins management he was ready to play that night.

Meanwhile, players were constantly shuffled back and forth from the minors as the Penguins used a team-record 48 players.

"I don't care what E.J. says—and I love him to death—but there were obviously machinations going on involving what was going to happen as we got closer to the draft," recalled then-vice president of marketing Tom Rooney.

The Penguins went 3-13 in March, and Johnston had his man. The Penguins finished with 38 points, New Jersey with 41. The Devils openly questioned the Penguins' policies late in the year.

Johnston didn't care. He was ready to draft the man who would save Penguins hockey.

"For once, we control our own destiny," Johnston said at the time. "The impact that Lemieux is going to have on our franchise is something we need. It won't just be the Pittsburgh Penguins; it will be Mario Lemieux and the Pittsburgh Penguins."

BUFFALO STAMPEDE

Marty McSorley witnessed more unusual things than most rookies, because he broke in with the 1983-84 Penguins, one of the worst teams of the modern era.

No sight was more curious than that of Gary Rissling squaring off with Larry Playfair, who often did not play fair.

Rissling stood 5-foot-9, 175 pounds. Playfair was 215. The 6-2 McSorley intervened, and managed to bring Playfair to his knees.

Rissling's eyes lit up.

"Riz looked at it like, 'Oh, boy, now he's my size,'" McSorley said. "He went right after him."

"Not one of my finer moments," said Rissling, who'd been teammates with Playfair in the AHL.

All three wound up in the penalty box.

"Big Larry leans on the glass, leans over the timekeepers and yells, 'Rissling, I'm going to kill ya,'" McSorley said. "So Riz pulls himself up over the glass—his head is barely over—and starts yelling back. The referee comes over and says, 'All three of you are out of here!' Riz is all smiles. I'm like, 'Oh my goodness.'"

SOUR GRAPES

Don Cherry, also known as "Grapes," would briefly be considered for the Penguins' coaching job in 1980, only a year after he became Enemy No. 1 at the Civic Arena.

Fans hung Cherry's bull terrier, Blue, in effigy, as Cherry's Boston Bruins were dismantling the Penguins in a second-round playoff series.

"I don't mind them wishing me or one of my players to die," Cherry told the *Pittsburgh Press.* "But to say something like that about a defenseless dog like my Blue is senseless."

ALMOST FAMOUS

Seven years after their crushing playoff loss to the New York Islanders, in which they blew a three-games-to-none lead, the Penguins had a chance to return the favor.

The Islanders had achieved great things after the 1975 series. They were the two-time defending Stanley Cup champions going into this first-round, best-of-five series in 1982, but the Penguins shocked the hockey world by erasing a two-games-to-none deficit and forcing Game 5 on Long Island.

There had been a 43-point difference between the teams during the regular season, so it was hard to believe that the Penguins took a 3-1 lead in Game 5 and held it as the clock wound down near the six-minute mark.

The Penguins were riding the wave of a smashing 5-2 victory in Game 4 back in Pittsburgh.

"I'll never forget [announcer] Mike Lange, after we won Game 4, said, 'You gotta believe,'" winger Paul Gardner said. "And when we went to the Island for Game 5 and came out for warm-up, there were huge signs from our fans who'd driven there, saying, 'You gotta believe.' It was a special time."

It was until the Islanders scored twice in the final six minutes, anyway. John Tonelli tied it with 2:21 left when a dump-in banked off

The Islanders broke the Penguins' hearts many times, including John Tonelli's series-winning, overtime goal in 1982. *(Photo courtesy of the Pittsburgh Penguins)*

the end-boards and popped over the stick of Penguins defenseman Randy Carlyle.

Tonelli picked it up in the slot and beat goaltender Michel Dion, who'd played spectacularly. Twenty-two years later, Carlyle still couldn't believe it.

"It was like God had flipped it over my stick," he said.

"Randy used a big, wide blade, too," teammate Greg Malone said later.

At 6:19 of overtime, Tonelli won it.

Carlyle was directly involved on a series-deciding goal the year before against St. Louis, when a centering pass deflected off his stick to Blues forward Mike Crombeen.

Carlyle, who'd mistakenly gone to the corner on the play, refused to blame bad luck.

"It was a bad brain cramp," he said.

LINESMAN THROWS A CHECK

Somehow, Gary Rissling carved a professional hockey career out of his 5-foot-9, 175-pound frame.

He did so by playing with the energy of a crazed animal.

"He'd stick his chin out to guys and say, 'You can't cut me! You can't cut scar tissue!'" recalled teammate Marty McSorley.

Rissling racked up 832 penalty minutes playing for the Penguins between 1980-85. He remained in the organization until 1987.

His colorful personality made him a natural for television ads. In one, he chewed a cup to pieces.

In a game one night, he was checked by a linesman.

Referees often tried to hold back the gritty Gary Rissling, who once took an elbow from a linesman. *(Photo courtesy of the Pittsburgh Penguins)*

"It was in St. Louis, and I was, as usual, on the bench chirping," Rissling recalled. "There was a linesman—I won't mention his name—who got tired of it. He came by the boards and ran into me, bending my arm over the boards. I was hurt, and back then, you didn't want to tell the trainer, 'I just got injured by the linesman.'"

Rissling fumed. The linesman no doubt realized his mistake.

"The rest of the game, he skated on the other side of the ice," Rissling said.

HEARTBREAKER

Former Penguins centerman Greg Malone described it as the sort of series where you "woke up with sore muscles you didn't even know you had."

The Penguins were huge underdogs against the St. Louis Blues in 1981 but forced the best-of-five series to the deciding game in St. Louis. The guy who won it in the second overtime hadn't even played in the first overtime.

Blues forward Mike Crombeen became ill in the third period, then made the Penguins sick all summer with a goal at 5:16 of the second overtime at the raucous Checkerdome in St. Louis.

Penguins goaltender Greg Millen, who would later play for the Blues, drew smiles during the games in St. Louis when he danced in his goal crease to the Budweiser theme song.

Millen also made 48 saves in Game 5, his last game in a Penguins sweater. Malone wound up playing on the same team with Crombeen in Hartford.

"He couldn't even take a puck and flip it on his stick," Malone said, laughing. "I saw him trying it one practice, and I went by and said, 'You scored the goal to beat us?'"

MONEY-BACK GUARANTEE

After his team lost the first two games of a best-of-five, first-round series to the mighty New York Islanders in 1982—by a combined score of 15-3—Penguins owner Edward J. DeBartolo offered fans a refund on tickets purchased for Game 3 and said he would not attend the game.

"We took that fairly personally," defenseman Randy Carlyle said. "I can remember [coach] Eddie Johnston coming back and challenging me, specifically, after Game 2. It was a heated

The Pens and the Blues shake hands after the Pens' crushing defeat in a 1981 series. *(Photo courtesy of the Pittsburgh Penguins)*

conversation. We weren't competing against the defending Stanley Cup champs."

DeBartolo's statement motivated the fans, too. Only about 200 or so took him up on his offer, and when the Penguins took the ice for Game 3, they were greeted with a standing ovation from a boisterous crowd of 14,310.

Intended or not, DeBartolo's pledge had worked to unite everyone against him … and in favor of his team.

"It was like people were saying, 'They're our team, and we'll be the ones to criticize them if they need to be criticized. They were our team before you got here, and they'll be our team when you leave,'" recalled Tom Rooney, then the team's vice president of marketing. "I know he didn't do it as a ploy, but it worked."

The Penguins won the next two games before losing a heartbreaking Game 5, in overtime, on Long Island.

BIG MISTAKE

Goaltender Greg Millen was one of the NHL's first restricted free agents to switch teams. Thing is, he never wanted to leave Pittsburgh.

After Millen turned in a memorable performance in the 1981 playoffs against St. Louis, the Hartford Whalers came along with a contract offer. Millen, then 24, and his agent immediately sent a similar proposal to the Penguins, expecting them to match Hartford's offer.

"I wanted to stay in Pittsburgh very badly," Millen said. "Hartford knew it would be matched."

It wasn't, because Penguins GM Baz Bastien had gone on vacation, and nobody in the Penguins' front office had been informed of the situation.

On the morning of the press conference in Hartford that would announce Millen's signing, Penguins president Paul Martha called him at a Hartford hotel.

Martha:I hear you're signing with Hartford.

Millen: We're not signing. We have signed.

Martha: What do you mean?

Millen: We gave Baz a contract, and he never responded to it.

Martha: What if we offer you U.S. Steel?

Millen: You can offer us whatever you want. The deal's done.

Martha later confirmed the foul-up. To this day, Millen wonders what might have been.

"It was too bad," he said. "We tried to stay."

The Penguins received decent compensation in the form of forwards Pat Boutette and Kevin McClelland.

FERGY FLIER

The third overtime game in Penguins history produced one of the more memorable finishes—and the fastest victory.

After goalie Denis Heron made the last of his 38 stops in the deciding Game 3 of a playoff series against the Buffalo Sabres, Gregg Sheppard whipped the rebound off the boards, into open ice.

George Ferguson, a.k.a. "The Fergy Flier," snatched it and sped down the left wing at Buffalo's Memorial Auditorium.

By the time his rush was finished, the Penguins had a 4-3 victory.

"I remember it vividly," Ferguson said. "It was such a big goal and such a big upset. Greg Sheppard cleared it, I anticipated it was coming out and took off. I had a lot of speed going down the left wing. A lot of the Sabres were caught napping. I remember going in on the off-wing and cutting to the middle for a better angle."

Everyone remembers Ferguson stuffing a shot past Bob Sauve. It would be the Penguins' last playoff series win until 1989.

THE GREAT TEMPTATION

In 1971, the Penguins began a not-so-grand tradition of trading away their first draft pick. They did it again in 1972, '77, '78, '79, '81 and '83 and had all of three playoff series victories to show for it.

Yet, several people in the organization wanted general manager Eddie Johnston to deal the No. 1 overall pick in 1984, which was clearly going to be French Canadian sensation Mario Lemieux.

There were some awfully tempting offers. Minnesota GM Lou Nanne, for example, offered all 12 of his team's picks, not that any after the first one or two would have meant much.

"I said, 'Lou, if you [offered all your draft picks] for the next three years in a row, I still wouldn't trade him,'" Johnston said. "If it wasn't for Mario, there wouldn't be a franchise here now. And if we would have traded him, it would have been an injustice to the city of Pittsburgh."

The Quebec Nordiques dangled the three Stastny brothers, Peter, Anton and Marian. The Montreal Canadiens, like Quebec desperate for hometown hero Lemieux, tried to sway Johnston with various combinations of players.

Johnston, himself a Montreal native, was the most popular guy in the league in the days leading up the draft.

And he never considered trading Lemieux. Not for an instant.

Johnston had scouted Lemieux himself and knew a rare talent when he saw one. He had, after all, played for the Boston Bruins when Bobby Orr came along.

Johnston listened to his higher-ups but refused to indulge their wishes.

"I just told them, 'I'm not dealing him,'" Johnston said. "There were some people who were saying we can get a lot of good players, but I remember [owner Edward J. DeBartolo] saying to me later, 'Thank God you didn't listen.'

"This place would be a parking lot."

3
WAITING TO WIN
(1984-1990)

TABLE HOCKEY

Talk about a buzz kill. About 1,500 Penguins fans excitedly watched the 1984 NHL Draft on closed-circuit TV at the Civic Arena, only to see top pick Mario Lemieux, on the advice of his agents, break tradition and refuse to approach the Penguins' table when his name was announced.

Lemieux, embroiled in a contract dispute, also refused to wear a Penguins jersey for publicity photos (he later said he regretted both moves).

Typical Penguins, many fans thought.

"The next day, we were flooded with phone calls from season-ticket holders," recalled then-vice president of marketing Tom Rooney. "They were saying, 'I'll sign when he signs.'"

Within days, Lemieux signed the largest rookie contract in NHL history, worth some $700,000.

A VIEW FOR LEMIEUX

The *New York Times* once called Pittsburgh "the only city with an entrance." There is no hint of a metropolis even as one drives to within a few hundred yards of it, on the Parkway West from the airport.

A hill blocks the spectacular skyline, which dramatically greets visitors as they emerge from the Fort Pitt Tunnel.

Paul Steigerwald, then a Penguins marketer, remembers when Mario Lemieux first laid on eyes on his new kingdom in the summer of 1984. Steigerwald had been dispatched to pick up Lemieux, plus Lemieux's father and agent, at the airport shortly after the NHL Draft.

Lemieux was 18.

"I prepped him for the view, and his eyes lit up when we went through the tunnel," Steigerwald said. "He could understand English, but he didn't want to speak it much. He just nodded his head.

"Even then, he had a touch of royalty about him."

FAST START

It took rookie center Mario Lemieux all of one shift to make an indelible mark on the National Hockey League. On October 11, 1984, at the fabled Boston Garden, he accidentally blocked a point shot by future Hall of Fame defenseman Raymond Bourque, skated in on a breakaway and deked goaltender Pete Peeters out of his jock before tucking the puck into an open net.

First game, first shift, first shot, first goal.

"Pete went one way, Mario went the other," recalled Eddie Johnston, the man who drafted Lemieux. "On the first shift of training camp, he did the same thing. He got the puck, went through the whole team and scored. First exhibition game, same thing.

"So, it didn't surprise me when he did that. But I think everybody else was in awe."

And would be for years to come.

SORRY

Mike Lange's most embarrassing moment as Voice of the Penguins?

Easy: The night he expressed on-air condolences to the family of the supposedly deceased Warren Riefer, events coordinator at the Civic Arena.

Riefer was still alive.

The problem began when arena employee Elaine Heufelder heard from a co-worker about Riefer's "death" and asked Lange if he would mention it during the Penguins' telecast that night.

Riefer was a familiar figure at the arena, busily navigating the halls on a golf cart. He was gravely ill at the time and would die within

Mario Lemieux reacts after scoring his first NHL goal—on his first shot—on October 12, 1984, in Boston. Pete Peeters is the goaltender. *(AP/WWP)*

weeks, but he was watching the game from his hospital bed when Lange mentioned his name.

"I said, 'We'll miss him, and we express condolences to family and friends,'" Lange said. "Next day, I get a call. He's not dead. He was watching the broadcast, and he almost lost it he laughed so hard. I think he even sent me a note saying how much he enjoyed it.

"At that time, I made a decision: I would have to see the person in the box to be able to say they had died."

LEMIEUX DEBUT

Ex-Vancouver Canucks winger Gary Lupul had a respectable NHL career but is remembered most for one thing: eating Mario Lemieux's fists.

"My nephews pulled my name up on the Internet, and it shows Mario giving me an uppercut," Lupul told the *Pittsburgh Tribune-Review*. "I played 300 games in the league, and I'm 40th in Canucks history in scoring, and a lot of people only remember that."

How could they forget?

It was a rainy night in Pittsburgh on October 17, 1984, Mario Lemieux's first home game. The Penguins' public relations staff billed it "The Lemieux Debut."

Lemieux set up a goal 18 seconds into what would become a 4-3 victory. Right after that, the 5-foot-9 Lupul started hounding Lemieux, who was seven inches taller.

Lupul slashed Lemieux and pushed him and finally speared him at the three-minute mark.

People questioned whether Lemieux would be able—or at least willing—to protect himself. He answered emphatically. He whipped off his gloves and buried Lupul in a flurry of punches that stunned everyone in the building.

Who expected this? The fans went bonkers.

This was like football!

"Right away, he was a hero to Pittsburgh fans because he was a tough guy, too," recalled Mike Lange, who called the game on television.

"I would say I got in about 10 uppercuts," Lemieux said after the game.

In the other dressing room, an embittered Lupul fired back the only way he could—with words.

"If he plays like that in this league," Lupul said, "he'll never last."

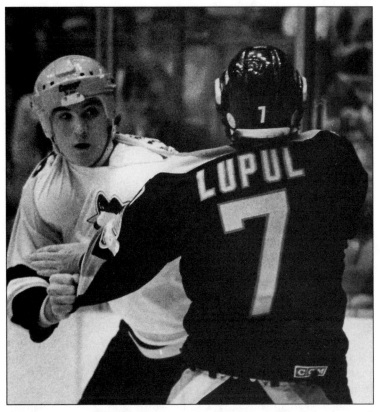

Mario Lemieux proved in his first home game—"The Lemieux Debut"—that he wasn't afraid to drop the gloves, here pounding Vancouver's Gary Lupul.
(Photo courtesy of the Pittsburgh Penguins)

BOTTOMS UP

Penguins coaches used to walk across the ice before games, through the players, on their way to the bench.

Veteran defenseman Bryan Maxwell apparently ended that routine.

Former teammate Warren Young recalled that Maxwell was not a big fan of head coach Bob Berry. During the warm up one night, Maxwell timed a fake fall perfectly, sliding underneath Berry and knocking him to the ice.

"That's why coaches today walk around the end, along the boards," Young said. "It was because of Maxy. Some other guys might tell that story differently, but that's how I remember it."

SNAPPING A JINX

The Penguins had gone 15 years and 42 games (0-39-3) without a victory at the Spectrum in Philadelphia entering their matchup there on February 2, 1989.

It had been so long that their most recent victory occurred with maskless Andy Brown in goal.

Head coach Gene Ubriaco decided to play back-up goaltender Wendell Young over Tom Barrasso, figuring maybe a former Flyer such as Young could help break the streak (When the Flyers traded Young the year before, owner Ed Snider said to him, "My fear is that you'll come back to haunt us.")

Others were way more superstitious than Ubriaco. Radio station 3-WS collected good-luck charms that ranged from cakes to old jerseys to women's undergarments.

"A lot of weird stuff," recalled 3-WS sportscaster Tab Douglas, who still has Young's stick from the game. "The most interesting thing a guy gave me was a little piece of yellow plastic. He said, 'I've been carrying that thing around for 10 years as a good luck charm.' It was a piece of a seat from the upper deck in Three Rivers Stadium, where Willie Stargell hit a home run that cracked a seat."

Injured Penguins Randy Cunneyworth and Zarley Zalapaski helped collect the items at a public free-for-all outside the arena. Douglas drove the box of trinkets to Philadelphia and dropped it in the Penguins' dressing room after their morning skate.

Invoking the supernatural as a way to win in Philly was nothing new—forwards Rob Brown and Phil Bourque had jokingly tried hypnosis for a game earlier in the year—but on this day, the madness reached a new level.

Pittsburgh radio hosts Scott Paulsen and Jim Krenn of WDVE-FM did their afternoon show from the Spectrum press box dressed as witch doctors, and Bourque wore his girlfriend's garter belt under his hockey pants.

It worked. Or something did. Young made 39 saves. John Cullen, Bourque, Bob Errey, Troy Loney and Dan Quinn scored the goals in a 5-3 victory.

Somebody suggested to Ubriaco that his team finally got the monkey off its back.

"More like a gorilla," he said.

CRAWL SPACE

When a talented Penguins team got off to a rough start in 1989, fans targeted head coach Gene Ubriaco, who dealt with the criticism creatively.

Ubriaco began walking under the stands to the bench so as to avoid catcalls. He climbed through a small doorway to get to his spot behind the players.

"Yup, he had a little trap door, and I remember him coming out from crawling underneath the bench, wiping all the peanuts off his suit and saying, 'Let's go, guys,'" winger Rob Brown said. "We eventually looked to see what he had to crawl through to get there. It was pretty disgusting."

One night, equipment manager Steve Latin remembered, Ubriaco crawled to his trap door only to find it locked. Ubriaco pounded on the door during the national anthem before somebody finally let him in.

Was it an accident?

"Well, we just kind of left him there for a little bit," Latin said. "He thinks it was an accident."

GREAT TRADE

Former NHL goaltending great Tony Esposito lasted only 106 games as Penguins general manager, but he made an important contribution to the two Stanley Cup championships that occurred shortly after his departure.

Esposito brought Tom Barrasso to Pittsburgh.

"Here's the way I put it," said Wendell Young, one of Barrasso's back-ups. "Mario won the Conn Smythe [as playoff MVP] two years in a row, but Tommy could just as easily have won. There were two key guys on the team: Mario and Tommy."

Esposito sent defenseman Doug Bodger and left winger Darrin Shannon—the No. 4 pick overall in 1988—to Buffalo for Barrasso and a third-round draft choice.

Tom Barrasso brought championship-caliber goaltending to Pittsburgh.
(Photo courtesy of the Pittsburgh Penguins)

It might have been the greatest trade in Penguins history. Barrasso had won a Vezina Trophy as a 19-year-old in Buffalo and was looking to recapture his mojo.

The Penguins needed a stopper.

"Tony knew goaltenders," said former Penguins president Paul Martha. "And he'd say, 'You can't win a Stanley Cup without a great goalkeeper. That's proven year after year.'"

The Penguins depended heavily on Barrasso, who set an NHL record with a 14-game postseason winning streak. The first 11 victories came in the 1992 playoffs against the New York Rangers, the Boston Bruins and the Chicago Blackhawks.

Barrasso was 16-5 with a 2.82 goals-against average in the playoffs that year, leading the team to its second consecutive Cup. The previous season, he was 12-7 with a 2.60 goals-against average. That included an 8-0 shutout victory at Minnesota in a Cup-clinching Game 6, when the Penguins were outshot 39-28.

Young had been acquired before Barrasso, with considerably less fanfare. Coach Gene Ubriaco advised Esposito to acquire Young, who was coming off a great playoff run in the American Hockey League.

Esposito's response: "Who the hell is Wendell Young?"

CHICKEN EGGS

Long before Ville Nieminen, the Penguins had another Finn named Ville. Both made interesting use of the English language.

Ville Siren was a defenseman who came along in 1984, when European players were scarce in the NHL. Veteran defenseman Moe Mantha took Siren under his wing. The two went everywhere together.

Siren struggled to convey his thoughts in English, so whenever Mantha ordered at a restaurant, Siren would say, "Same as him."

One morning in New York, Mantha set Siren free.

"I said to him, 'You're on your own today,'" Mantha recalled. "When the waitress asked him what he wanted, he said, 'I'll have eggs and bacon and toast.'"

And when the waitress asked Siren what kind of eggs he wanted, he said, "Chicken."

FLYING TELEVISION

Former Penguins television analyst Paul Steigerwald couldn't remember the exact date. Understandably so, considering what happened:

A replay monitor dropped from its perch and clipped the side of his head and shoulder, causing a mid-sentence shut down as he and Mike Lange called a game.

"Mike just glanced at me, shook his head in disbelief and continued to call the game as if nothing had happened," Steigerwald said. "Eventually, he told the viewers, 'A TV monitor just fell on Staggy's head,' and asked if I was OK.

"I cracked the obligatory joke about needing a helmet in the booth and went about my work, realizing that I could have been seriously injured if I had been sitting six inches to my right.

"Imagine your 17-inch television landing on your head, and you'll get the picture."

PIERRE CREAMER

Let the record show that Pierre Creamer, in his only season as Penguins coach (1987-88), produced the team's best winning percentage in nine years.

Let it also show that the mostly French-speaking Creamer confused an awful lot of people, including his players.

For proof, refer to the second-last game of the season.

The Penguins needed to win to keep their playoff hopes alive, but Creamer thought his team needed only a tie and failed to pull his goaltender as time wound down in a 6-6 deadlock with the Washington Capitals.

"We were on the bench, and [forward] Dave Hunter was yelling to Pierre, 'We need to win!'" winger Rob Brown recalled. "We were all turning around, saying, 'Are you going to pull our goalie?'

"[Creamer] was calling upstairs and was convinced we needed a tie, but somebody told him that was wrong."

Finally, Creamer called timeout—and proceeded to speak French with star center Mario Lemieux while the other five players on the ice stared blankly at each other.

"We're like, 'Ah, Pierre, we don't speak French,'" Brown said. "I'm sure he said to Mario, 'Go end to end and win the game,' and that's exactly what happened."

penguique...

eyetique

Mike Lange and Paul Steigerwald had some memorable moments in the broadcast booth. *(Photo courtesy of the Pittsburgh Penguins)*

Lemieux scored a remarkable goal while falling on his back. The Penguins missed the playoffs, anyway. Gene Ubriaco replaced Creamer after the season.

Brown had another memory of Creamer. It was Brown's first year, and Creamer called him into his office near the end of training camp.

"He said, 'Rob, we like you, but we think you're our No. 6 center; we're going to send you to junior,'" Brown said. "I said, 'I can't go to

GM Eddie Johnston (right) introduces Pierre Creamer, who wore the coaching cap for one unforgettable season. *(Photo courtesy of the Pittsburgh Penguins)*

junior.' He said, 'How old are you?' I said, '19,' which made me too old.

"So he says, 'OK, you'll start the season here.' Well, all righty then."

Brown had 24 goals in 51 games that year, fourth best on the team.

MAKING A BIKE

Head coach Pierre Creamer was incensed one morning, ex-goaltender Gilles Meloche recalled, and kicked his players off the ice. Creamer ordered them to ride exercise bikes, only his words weren't clear.

A French-Canadian, Creamer sometimes mangled his English, especially when he was mad. His exact words to the players that day were, "Go make a bike!"

The players proceeded to draw a bicycle on the chalkboard and head home.

MARKETING MARIO

Bob Berry's arrival as Penguins coach in 1984 coincided with Mario Lemieux's arrival as franchise savior. This wasn't always a good thing, at least not for the marketing department.

Berry was an old-time hockey guy who'd come from Montreal, where no marketing of the local hockey club was necessary.

It was critical in Pittsburgh. Attendance the year before Lemieux arrived was 6,839 per game with exactly zero sellouts. Berry figured a winner would take care of attendance problems.

In the meantime, he didn't have much time—or patience—for promotions.

"We used to battle with Bob all the time about doing things like taking Mario from practice to some grand opening of a Burger King or something," recalled then-vice president of marketing, Tom Rooney, who immediately seized on the fact that Lemieux's last name, in French, means "The Best."

"Mario, at that point in time, didn't know any better."

Everywhere Pittsburghers looked, there was Lemieux. Fans could buy a Mario Lemieux Growth Chart, and *Sports Illustrated* made him do a photo shoot at the Pittsburgh Zoo, where he was photographed among live penguins.

One day, marketing director Paul Steigerwald poked his head into Berry's office to inform him that *Evening Magazine*, a local television show, wanted to bring a live penguin to practice for a photo shoot.

"Well, keep the [expletive] thing away from me," Berry grumbled.

It didn't get any better as the season wore on.

Said Rooney: "We got in more and more trouble."

HEXTALL'S FURY

Rob Brown wasn't even that excited about his goal, because the game was out of hand.

Philadelphia Flyers goalie Ron Hextall was pretty hyped, though.

Brown, known for hot-dog celebrations, had put the Penguins ahead 9-2 in Game 5 of a first-round, best-of-seven series against the hated Flyers. As he went to hug teammate Dan Quinn, he saw Hextall charging his way with his stick raised above his head.

Hextall—the son of former Penguins defenseman Bryan Hextall—seemed intent on decapitating Brown, who wasn't the world's fastest skater but quickly found a new gear. He took a U-turn and sped out of harm's way.

The incident made for one of the more memorable video clips in Penguins history.

"I'll never forget the look on Danny Quinn's face when I skated away from him as he was about to hug me," Brown said. "It was like, 'Where are you going?' It was probably the quickest I've ever skated in my life.

"Whenever I see somebody from Pittsburgh, that's always the thing they ask me about. They'll never forget it. Neither will I."

The goal, incidentally, wound up being important, because the Flyers stormed back before losing, 10-7. Philadelphia won the last two games of the series to hand the Penguins yet another crushing playoff defeat.

CIRCUS PERFORMERS

The Penguins began the 1986-87 season by winning seven consecutive games. The giddiness soon wore off, and by March, Coach Bob Berry was ready to strangle somebody.

Namely, his players.

Berry let loose March 5 after a 7-2 loss at home to the Toronto Maple Leafs. It came two days after an 8-1 win at Quebec. His postgame tirade took an immediate place of prominence among all-time Penguin meltdowns.

"Win one, 8-1, lose one, 7-2—easy come, easy go," Berry fumed. "That's the [expletive] attitude we had tonight. They don't have the [expletive] intestinal fortitude. Big shots. In the back door, put the [expletive] show on, back out on the bus, go somewhere else, just like circus performers.

"They tell everybody they're professional hockey players. They might be [expletive] hockey players, but they're not very [expletive] professional.

"That's all I've got to say."

VALIANT EFFORT

On Valentine's Day, 1990, Mario Lemieux was pierced to the heart. Lemieux had picked up at least one point in each of the

Coach Bob Berry once labeled his team "circus performers."
(Photo courtesy of the Pittsburgh Penguins)

previous 46 games, the second-longest streak in NHL history behind Wayne Gretzky's 51.

Lemieux fought crippling back pain during much of the streak. It finally forced him out of a game against the New York Rangers in the second period.

"It's tough to accept," he said afterward. "But that's the way it goes."

Earlier in the season, equipment manager Steve Latin had carpenters make a special contraption—similar to something one would find in a shoestore—that allowed Lemieux to tie his skates without bending his back.

"He was having so many problems just putting his skates on," Latin recalled. "Just standing up was a chore."

MAGIC STICK

Things were not going well for right winger Ron Duguay in 1986. A one-time 40-goal scorer, his career was in decline, and he was mired in a lengthy slump.

Former teammate Bob Errey picks up the story from there.

"He hadn't scored in a dozen games or so," Errey said. "We were in New York and went to this bar in Manhattan. He sees one of his sticks on the wall—one he'd scored a hat trick with 10 years earlier with the Rangers—and grabs it off the wall."

Duguay used the stick the next night against the Islanders.

Needless to say, he scored.

"Somebody dumped it in on the left boards. It hit a partition, and the goalie went back to play it, but it came out in front," Errey said, laughing. "Doogs was all alone. He put it in the wide-open net. He was dancing around.

"After the game, his stick representative was there, and Doogs had them make a few dozen sticks in that exact same pattern."

Duguay's luck didn't last. He had only 11 goals in 53 games with the Penguins and bounced around the NHL for a few more years before playing in the minors and eventually becoming a coach.

UNUSUAL ADVICE

Troy Loney played 532 games with the Penguins, few of which stood out more than his first. Loney, a left winger, had been recalled from the minors to play for Lou Angotti's wretched 1983-84 squad.

"During the warmup, Lou says to me, 'Look around here; there are a bunch of cancers,'" Loney said. "He says, 'Don't listen to these guys or behave like them.'"

Oh, and one more thing: Angotti wanted Loney to play right wing and asked if he'd ever played that position. Loney said no.

Angotti's response: "Well, good luck out there tonight."

CRAIG PATRICK

Born of royal hockey lineage—a member of the famous Patrick family—Craig Patrick was an assistant coach under Herb Brooks when the United States won a miraculous gold medal in 1980.

Patrick went on to produce 11 consecutive Penguins playoff teams and won two Stanley Cups after he was hired as the team's general manager on December 5, 1989.

But he started out like any other kid who loves sports.

If you walked into Patrick's bedroom in Wellesley, Massachusetts, around 1955, you'd find shoeboxes filled with baseball cards, stacked halfway up the walls.

If you walked outside, you might find Patrick firing a tennis ball against the garage. He was pretending to be his favorite team, the Detroit Tigers (he was born in Detroit).

He aimed between the windows of his parents' bedroom and waited for the ball to bounce back. If it eluded him, it was recorded as a single, double, or triple, depending on where it landed.

If it bounced over the wall behind him, it was a home run. Only a hard pitch could result in a homer, but even back then, Patrick found a way to make his team win.

"When the Tigers were up," he said, "I always threw a little harder."

If you could peak into one of his elementary school classes, you might see Patrick working at his desk. The assignments varied, the theme did not.

Always hockey.

Patrick's grandfather, Lester, already was a renowned NHL figure, one of the original builders of the game. Craig's father, Lynn, managed the Boston Bruins. Craig Patrick loved to watch games at the old Boston Garden. He sat in the same seats every time.

Not that any of this mattered to his teachers, who were concerned about his hockey obsession. They would send him home with written complaints pinned to his chest.

These were not anonymous teachers, either. One was the sister of hockey legend Art Ross, another the sister of Hall of Fame goalie Roy Worters.

"They complained, too," Patrick said.

CLASSIC TAPE

Little did Tracy Luppe know that when he arrived at the Civic Arena on New Year's Eve, 1988, he would become a part of hockey history.

A small part, to be sure, but a part nonetheless.

Mario Lemieux celebrates one of his five goals against New Jersey on New Year's Eve, 1988, the night he became the only player in NHL history to score every type of goal in a game. *(Photo courtesy of the Pittsburgh Penguins)*

Mario Lemieux that night became the only player in NHL history to score each type of goal—even-strength, power-play, short-handed, penalty shot and empty-net—in the same game.

Lemieux's last goal of the night (the empty-netter) appeared to occur slightly after time had elapsed in an 8-6 victory over the New Jersey Devils, but who wanted to spoil such a celebratory moment on New Year's Eve?

Certainly not Luppe, who, for the first time, taped Lemieux's sticks before the game that night. Luppe had been working for the team for four years.

"Mario said, 'Hey, you want to tape my sticks?'" Luppe recalled in 2004. "I'm like, 'What?' He says, 'Yeah, you want to tape my sticks?' Well, he goes out and gets five goals five different ways. Needless to say, I'm still doing them today."

When new players join the Penguins, they take note of the fact that Luppe prepares each of Lemieux's four sticks before every game.

"A few guys are like, 'Hey, tape my sticks; see if it rubs off,'" Luppe said.

THE 'OTHER' LEMIEUX

Alain Lemieux, Mario's younger brother, played exactly one game for the Penguins, during the 1986-87 season.

Mario Lemieux wore No. 66, of course, which led equipment man John Doolan to jokingly offer Alain Lemieux No. 33 when he joined the team.

"I teased him that he was only half as good as his brother," Doolan said.

Alain Lemieux wore No. 11 that night. His older brother was injured and did not play.

SINGE-ING THE BLUES

By the end of the 2003-04 season, Mario Lemieux had played only 26 games in 16 seasons against the St. Louis Blues but had somehow managed 25 goals and 58 points.

What's more, he had recorded games of two goals, three goals, four goals, five goals, seven points and eight points against St. Louis—and that didn't include the 1988 All-Star Game at St. Louis, when he scored three goals and set up three others.

"Ridiculous," said Lemieux's former teammate, Ian Moran. "I just get really disappointed when he gets more goals in one game than I get in a season."

There's more.

Lemieux recorded his first career hat trick against St. Louis (a four-goal effort on New Year's Eve, 1985), and the Blues are the only team that pops up on his personal-record list for goals, assists, and points.

He scored five goals three times, including once against the Blues on March 26, 1996, in an 8-4 victory in Wayne Gretzky's only appearance at the Civic Arena in a Blues sweater.

Lemieux dished out six assists three times, once against the Blues (October 15, 1988, in a 9-2 victory at the Civic Arena). That was one of the two eight-point games in his career.

Any explanation for this phenomenon?

"No," Lemieux said. "None whatsoever."

LONG STAY

Shortly after rookie defenseman Doug Bodger joined the Penguins in 1984, he was living out of a Holiday Inn, so general manager Eddie Johnston called veteran Moe Mantha to ask a favor.

"E.J. says, 'Do you mind having this kid living with you for a month?'" Mantha recalled. "He stayed for two years. My wife helped him with a bank account and laundry. He paid her $200 a month to help him out.

"I used to joke that the only reason he ever moved out was because he was traded."

COFFEY BREAK

Tom McMillan was a beat writer covering the Penguins when they acquired defenseman Paul Coffey from Edmonton on November 24, 1987.

McMillan had watched the team since childhood and later became its vice president of communications and marketing. He'd never seen anything like Coffey, a three-time Stanley Cup winner who had three assists in his home debut, as the Penguins roared back from a 4-0 deficit in the final 25 minutes to defeat the Quebec Nordiques, 6-4, in overtime.

"The first time he got the puck and skated, you couldn't believe a Penguin was skating that fast," McMillan said. "At that point, you got

Defenseman Paul Coffey wore extra-small skates and dull blades—and, man, could he fly. *(Photo courtesy of the Pittsburgh Penguins)*

the sense they could actually be good. That started the avalanche of all these great players coming here.

"Before that, it was really only Mario."

GM Eddie Johnston engineered the deal, sending Craig Simpson, Dave Hannan, and Moe Mantha to Edmonton for Dave Hunter, Wayne Van Dorp, and Coffey, a three-time Stanley Cup winner who was mired in a contract holdout at the time.

Suddenly, Lemieux had a player who could create space, feed him pinpoint passes, and quarterback the left point on the power play.

The rest of the league was in trouble.

LINE DANCING

When former Penguins winger Luc Robitaille said a fire hydrant could score 40 goals on Mario Lemieux's line, everybody knew it was a gross exaggeration.

No way Lemieux could coax more than 20 goals out of a hydrant.

But the guys who have played on his lines will tell you that he took their games to never-imagined heights. They'll also tell you it was as much a challenge as it was a treat.

If it were easy to mesh with Lemieux's greatness, he wouldn't have gone through linemates like underwear his first several years. A guy can't just walk off the street and play a duet with George Winston or act a scene with Al Pacino in front of 17,000 people.

"You have to have a guy who's confident in his abilities, who has some self-worth," said Penguins radio analyst Bob Errey, a longtime Lemieux linemate.

Skating with Lemieux is the opportunity of a lifetime. Ask Warren Young, who scored 40 goals as a 28-year-old rookie journeyman, or Terry Ruskowski, who, at 31, had a career-best 26 goals next to Lemieux.

Ask Markus Naslund, who had 15 points in his first 85 NHL games, then scored 52 in 66 games with Lemieux.

Ask Jaromir Jagr, who had a personal-best 62 goals on Lemieux's right in 1995-96. Ask Errey, who had a career-best 26 goals in 1988-89, or Rob Brown, who had a career-high 115 points as a 20-year-old.

Lemieux's best line early in his career had Brown on the right and Errey on the left. In 1992-93, he formed a dynamic trio with Kevin Stevens and Rick Tocchet, then with Jagr and Ron Francis.

Early on, one of Lemieux's lines saw him skate with Ruskowski and Doug Shedden.

"[Lemieux] would say, 'Give me the puck and go to the net and keep your stick on the ice,'" Shedden recalled. "OK, that's easy enough."

How long did it take Brown to adjust?

"One game, because I wanted to stay there bad," he said. "I wanted to make sure I was ready. I remember we were driving back from the airport one day, and Ken Schinkel, the assistant GM, told me I'd be on Mario's line. I had a smile on my face the rest of the day."

JOHNNY ON THE SPOT

Through good times and bad, a familiar voice has rung through the rafters at Penguins games.

Public address announcer John Barbero, a bespectacled former high school English teacher (later a principal), and one-time radio voice of the American Basketball Association's Pittsburgh Pipers, started playing games with players' names early in his career.

Some players didn't like it.

"I dragged out the Z's on Zarley Zalapski, and he told me he was embarrassed," said Barbero, who started working games in the early 1970s. "He asked me not to do it anymore."

One day in the late 1980s, TV announcer Mike Lange said to Barbero, "Why don't you do something with Mario?"

Next game, Barbero belted out what became his signature call: "Pittsburgh goal scored by No. 66, Mario Lemiuewwwwwwww!"

Fans loved it.

How did Lemieux feel?

"He never said a word," Barbero said, "so I assumed he liked it."

RESCUE MISSION

Warren Young could have crumbled. Playing in front of family and friends in his hometown of Toronto, he was awarded a penalty shot on January 2, 1985, against the Maple Leafs.

Rookie center Mario Lemieux came to his rescue.

"Before I had a chance to be nervous, this 19-year-old kid tells me, 'Go with speed,'" said Young, then 29. "That became my focus."

Young scored against goaltender Tim Bernhardt, the second of nine consecutive penalty shot goals for the Penguins from 1984-1991 (five by Lemieux).

MUSIC TO THEIR EARS

Before ear-splitting acid rock made its way into hockey arenas, organists filled the breaks in action. Penguins organist Vince Lascheid was one of the best. His creative and well-timed ditties tickled the home fans and sometimes infuriated opponents and referees.

When gritty Penguins forward Pat Hickey went to the penalty box, Lascheid would crank out a Cole Porter tune called, "I've Got You Under My Skin."

When the referees came out before the game, Lascheid was liable to play "Three Blind Mice."

"Sometimes the songs were very poor," Lascheid said, "but at least it was something."

Other Lascheid classics:
- "The Godfather Theme Song"—off-key—directed at Boston Bruins superstar Phil Esposito.
- "Tommy" for Penguins goalie Tom Barrasso.
- "Anchors Aweigh" for Penguins enforcer Bob "Battleship" Kelly.
- Theme from the TV show "Bonanza" for fighter Steve Durbano.
- The Maxwell House jingle for defenseman Paul Coffey.
- "The Night Chicago Died" when the Penguins beat the Chicago Blackhawks.
- "Give My Regards To Broadway" when they beat the New York Rangers.
- "The Night The Lights Went Out In Georgia" when they beat the Atlanta Flames.

The NHL took offense to Lascheid playing "Three Blind Mice" and ordered him to quit, but he still sneaked it in every once a while "just to see what would happen."

Once, referee Paul Stewart called the press box to complain.

One of Lascheid's early classics was the homemade chant, "Let's Go Pronovost!" in honor of Penguins star Jean Pronovost. It was the counter-chant to Buffalo Sabres fans yelling, "Let's Go Buffalo!"

Sabres fans used to travel to Pittsburgh by the busload, making for a charged atmosphere at the Civic Arena.

"The Pronovost thing started when I was driving through the Liberty Tunnels one night," Lascheid said. "I started with my horn— Da-da-dadada. Lo and behold, everybody started honking their horns, too. It was a lot of fun."

MANTHA'S HOT TUB

In the mid-1980s, defenseman Moe Mantha had the most popular house on the team, complete with indoor shuffleboard, a bowling alley and a backyard hot tub.

Mantha recalls that youngsters Mario Lemieux, Doug Bodger, and Roger Belanger—the team's top three draft picks from 1984—would sometimes come over to sit in the hot tub and smoke cigars.

"Little 19-year-old rookies smoking cigars in the hot tub," Mantha recalled, laughing. "I've got pictures of it. If I ever need a job, I might call Mario and blackmail him, the skinny little runt."

STAR OF STARS

The NHL All-Star Game came to Pittsburgh on January 21, 1990, and it became the Mario Lemieux Show precisely 21 seconds after the opening faceoff. That was when Lemieux scored one of his four goals, joining Wayne Gretzky as the only NHL players to accomplish the feat to that point. In only his sixth season, Lemieux was named All-Star Game MVP for an unprecedented third time.

CRAZY MAN

Rob Brown was plain nuts when he played junior hockey. He would write messages to opposing players on the tape of his stick. He would goof off against inferior opponents.

And he would go to team parties dressed in his coach's pants.

That's right, Brown and his friend Mark Recchi, another future Penguin, each put their whole body in one of 500-pound coach Ken Hitchcock's pant legs. The two simultaneously shared one of Hitchcock's jackets, too. That's how they walked into a Kamloops team party together in 1986.

Hitchcock eventually lost weight and became an accomplished NHL coach.

Brown, too, experienced a remarkable transformation. Four seasons removed from scoring 115 points on a line with Mario Lemieux, he had no NHL contract and wound up in the minors. He worked his way back to the NHL several years later and re-invented himself as a checker under Penguins coach Kevin Constantine.

HIRING PATRICK

Craig Patrick was on the Penguins' radar more than a year before he was hired.

"I tried to get him to the Penguins earlier," said ex-team president Paul Martha. "I met with him a couple of times at LaGuardia Airport."

Patrick had been fired by the New York Rangers, but the Penguins hired Tony Esposito in April, 1988, on the orders of owner Edward J. DeBartolo. When Esposito was fired in December of 1989, Martha knew who to call.

"I'd done my homework," he said. "A lot of people felt Craig Patrick was the upcoming guy. I was able to convince Mr. [Edward] DeBartolo that Craig Patrick was really the right choice."

WINNER'S CIRCLE

Goaltender Wendell Young made Penguins history when he stopped 39 shots to help break the team's 15-year jinx at the Spectrum in Philadelphia. That wasn't his greatest feat, though.

This was: He is the only player to have won each of the following four championships in North American hockey: the Stanley Cup (Penguins, 1991 and '92); the American Hockey League's Calder Cup (Hershey Bears, 1988); the Canadian Major Junior's Memorial Cup (Kitchener Rangers, 1982); and the International Hockey League's Turner Cup (Chicago Wolves, 1998, 2000).

Nobody can equal the record, because the International League is extinct.

"It's an amazing thing with the little bit of talent I had," Young said.

His luck didn't stop when he joined the Wolves, who joined the AHL, as the executive director of team relations. The team won the Calder Cup in 2002, giving Young yet another ring.

WREGGET'S GAME 7

A smoker at the time, Philadelphia Flyers goaltender Ken Wregget was dying for a cigarette before Game 7 of a 1989 playoff series against the Penguins.

Wregget and Flyers trainer Kurt Mundt used to leave a pack of matches in a hidden spot at every arena so that when they went for a smoke, they had an easy light.

On this particular morning at the Civic Arena, Wregget had just been informed that starting goalie Ron Hextall couldn't play because of a bad knee.

Few favored the Flyers, playing a back-up goalie against the turbo-charged Penguins, who'd won Game 5 at the Civic Arena, 10-7.

Wregget, who would join the Penguins three years later, remembers waiting anxiously for the game to start.

"The nerves were phenomenal," he said. "I remember the hotel room, trying to sleep, seeing the big silver dome [of the Civic Arena] outside of my window. It was kind of ominous."

When Wregget finally got to the game, he was a basket case. Mundt calmed him down.

"He said, 'This is the stuff you dream about your whole life; you shouldn't be scared about it. Just relax and have fun,'" Wregget recalled. "I thought, 'He's right.'"

Wregget stoned the Penguins in a 4-1 victory.

NATURAL WONDER

Mario Lemieux wasn't sure he could play in Game 5 of a 1989 playoff series against the Philadelphia Flyers. He'd sustained a neck injury during Game 4 when he collided with teammate Randy Cunneyworth.

Well, Lemieux not only played, he tied three league records and set or tied 11 team records. He became the second player in NHL history to record five goals in a playoff game and the fourth to record eight points, as the Penguins won, 10-7, to take a three-games-to-two lead (they would lose the series).

Lemieux notched a natural hat trick in a span of four minutes 40 seconds, scoring on his second, third, and fourth shots against goalie Ron Hextall.

DRAFTING JAGR

The Penguins caught a break when the Philadelphia Flyers fired general manager Bobby Clarke on the eve the 1990 NHL Draft. Clarke coveted a talented Czechoslovakian winger named Jaromir Jagr.

So did Penguins GM Craig Patrick, who had seen Jagr at the World Championships, skating on the Czechs' third line with future NHLers Bobby Holik and Robert Reichel.

"We were hoping we would get him," Patrick said. "But we were real worried."

Other teams had their own concerns about Jagr. Some feared he wouldn't be able to get out of Czechoslovakia. Others were said to be leery of European players.

The Vancouver Canucks, drafting second overall in their home arena, opted for a Czech who had defected to North America—Petr Nedved—after the Quebec Nordiques took Owen Nolan with the first pick.

The Detroit Red Wings took Keith Primeau third, followed by the Flyers. Jagr later recalled his heart pounding as the Flyers prepared to announce their selection. He thought he was headed to Philadelphia, but the Flyers took forward Mike Ricci.

That left the Penguins to snag Jagr, who would be become one of the most dynamic offensive talents in NHL history.

"He was, by far, the best prospect," said Penguins head scout Greg Malone "We had to take him."

Patrick recalled that Jagr wanted to come to North America immediately, but to clinch the deal, Patrick flew Jagr and his parents to Pittsburgh after the draft.

"Craig showed him the city, let his parents see it so they would know what they were getting into," Malone said. "The plan was to get him here as quick as possible. At the end of the week, his parents were comfortable with letting him come."

The Penguins also had to pay Jagr's Czech team in Kladno $200,000.

Years later, a reporter asked Patrick the following question: "If somebody had asked you privately whether you were confident you'd get Jagr, what would you have said?"

Patrick's answer revealed plenty about his management style.

"I wouldn't have said anything," he said. "I wouldn't have let anybody know that's what we wanted."

PARTY TIME

When Jaromir Jagr first arrived in Pittsburgh, immediately after the 1990 NHL Draft, Penguins general manager Craig Patrick threw a small party at his apartment. Patrick invited several local Czechs and told Jagr that he could pick a family with whom to live.

Jagr, in his self-titled autobiography, remembered a late-arriving guest stealing the show. It was Mario Lemieux.

"Mario came up to me, extended his hand and said, 'If you need anything, you can always come to me. I was in the exact same situation you are now when I came to Pittsburgh speaking only French, and I still remember how hard it was. So, don't worry, I know the problems you'll be having, and I know how you're feeling. I'm ready to help you any time,'" Jagr recounted. "I had my picture taken with Mario that night, and to this day, whenever I look at that photograph, I remember what Mario said to me."

It was soon discovered that in jumbling the letters to Jaromir, one could create a rather appropriate anagram: Mario Jr.

HEY SONG

The expansion Colorado Rockies introduced the familiar "Hey Song" to the National Hockey League in the mid-1970s, but it had virtually disappeared from sports arenas before the Penguins revived it during a 1989 playoff series against the Philadelphia Flyers.

The familiar Gary Glitter song—actually titled "Rock & Roll, Part 2"—has since become an anthem of sorts in professional sports venues.

Former Penguins marketer Tinsy Labrie remembered her brother introducing her to the song. Chase Edmondson, who was in charge of music at the arena, liked it and agreed to play it.

Fans loved it.

Edmondson came up with another popular idea during the Stanley Cup years in 1991 and '92. When the Penguins went on a power play, he would play the theme to the movie *Jaws*. Fans would then wave yellow placards picturing shark fins.

THE PROMISE

Nobody was surprised when the Penguins added another heartbreaking chapter to their history on the final day of the 1989-90 season.

Needing a victory to beat the Buffalo Sabres, who'd been eliminated from the playoffs, the Penguins blew it when Sabres

Craig Patrick sits dejectedly in the media interview room on March 31, 1990, just after telling reporters his team would never miss the playoffs again, as it did that night on Buffalo's overtime goal. *(Photo by James M. Kubus/Pittsburgh Tribune-Review)*

defenseman Uwe Krupp beat Tom Barrasso from the left point in overtime.

After the game, a reporter suggested to new Penguins general manager Craig Patrick—also the team's interim coach—that this was typical of the hard-luck Penguins.

"That's going to change," Patrick snapped.

He went on to say that missing the playoffs "would never happen again."

On June 12 of that year, Patrick hired Bob Johnson as his new coach and Scotty Bowman as director of player development and recruitment.

Suddenly, the Penguins had the most feared management group in the NHL.

They would make the playoffs each of the next 11 years and win two Stanley Cups.

4
GLORY DAYS
(1991-1996)

HOW DO YOU LIKE US NOW?

Lovable losers for much of their first 24 years, the Penguins gained instant respect on June 12, 1990, when general manager Craig Patrick hired "Badger" Bob Johnson as coach and Scotty Bowman as director of player development.

Suddenly, the Penguins had three of the most respected names in hockey running their team.

Johnson's rampant optimism would help to transform the culture of hockey in Pittsburgh, and Bowman was the winningest coach in NHL history. He'd been working as an analyst with *Hockey Night in Canada* but was enticed to come to Pittsburgh because of Patrick, who called his new group "the best management team in the NHL."

Others took note.

"A pretty impressive front-end team," remarked Edmonton Oilers GM Glen Sather.

BADGER BOB

The Penguins were a fragile bunch when "Badger" Bob Johnson took the coaching reins in June of 1990.

New general manager Craig Patrick had phoned the 59-year-old Johnson the previous December from the Met Center in Minneapolis.

Johnson had been out of the NHL for three years but immediately said yes when Patrick asked if he'd be interested in coaching again.

Craig Patrick introduces his impressive new management team—coach Bob Johnson and director of player development, Scotty Bowman—on June 12, 1990.
(Photo by James M. Kubus/Pittsburgh Tribune-Review)

"Badger" Bob—the nickname came from his days coaching the Wisconsin Badgers—could not join the team until the following season because of obligations to USA Hockey, an entity with which Patrick was intimately familiar.

Patrick had been Herb Brooks' assistant coach with the 1980 U.S. Olympic Team that produced the Miracle on Ice (Johnson's son, Mark, was a star player on that team and later played for the Penguins).

Turning the Penguins into a champion would require a miracle of its own.

The team was coming off a season in which it was eliminated from playoff contention in its final regular-season game in overtime. It was one of many tortuous endings the franchise had suffered in its first 24 years.

Beginnings were often quite painful, too.

"We were teetering," winger Phil Bourque recalled. "We didn't know if we were going to be good or stink."

And they weren't sure what to make of the quirky Johnson, either.

"He was just such a character," defenseman Larry Murphy said. "When I first met him, he gave me this list of top 10 foods. He says, 'I want you to have this.' I remember the banana being No. 1. That sticks out in my mind."

• • •

One of Johnson's first moves was to hold training camp in Vail, Colorado.

Initially, players were bummed. There was nowhere to go, and the altitude made for rough training.

This was part of Johnson's plan.

"For the first few days, guys were puking over the boards because of the altitude," Bourque said. "They were just dying. But after we settled in with the atmosphere and everything, it definitely helped us with our conditioning."

Players became closer because they were virtually forced to spend time together. They went mountain biking and hiking and hung out at night.

Eight months later, they would still be hanging out—at a raucous Stanley Cup celebration at the Met Center in Minneapolis, the same place where Craig Patrick had first contacted "Badger" Bob Johnson.

• • •

Johnson's players loved him because he always had their best interests in mind. This was never truer than during the final game of the 1990-91 season, when the New York Rangers couldn't figure out why the Penguins' bench was so enthusiastic late in a meaningless, 6-3 Rangers victory.

The Penguins had clinched a playoff spot and had nothing at stake that day at Madison Square Garden. Not as a team, anyway. Certain players had contract bonuses on the line.

Late in the game, Johnson shouted to his players on the bench: "Anybody have any bonuses for points or goals?"

Randy Gilhen needed a goal for a $20,000 bonus, so Johnson repeatedly sent him on the ice. In the final minute, Gilhen went out on a power play and scored.

"It was the first time I ever played the power play there," Gilhen recalled. "The greatest thing about Badger was that he instilled so much confidence in the guys. He had you believing you could do anything."

Whether he was working with NHL players or Pee Wees, "Badger" Bob Johnson loved to teach. *(Photo courtesy of the Pittsburgh Penguins)*

• • •

Never one to adhere to convention, Johnson had his players work out in a hotel ballroom the morning of a 1991 playoff game in Boston.

He was eager to test a new breakout.

"He used pucks on the floor," defenseman Larry Murphy recalled. "We were wearing street clothes, and guys were swinging around behind the chairs, working on the breakout. There was never a dull moment back then."

• • •

In five years coaching the Calgary Flames, Johnson came close but did not win a Stanley Cup, so he knew it was the opportunity of a lifetime going into Game 6 of the 1991 final in Minneapolis, the city where he was born.

Veteran forward Joe Mullen, whom Johnson brought to Pittsburgh, remembered seeing Johnson and his wife, Martha, in the corridors before the game.

"They said, 'You have a Cup already. We need this one,'" Mullen said. "I said, 'We'll get it.'"

FLAT ON HIS BACK

All the hope the Penguins carried into the 1990-91 season seemed to disappear during a preseason road trip to Houston, where Mario Lemieux's back pain literally dropped him to his knees.

Lemieux was coming off surgery to repair a herniated disk. It was discovered the next day that he had a rare disc-space infection. He would lay flat on his back for the next three months and would miss the first 50 games.

"It was a difficult time, lying there on my back, knowing I had an infection that was very serious and could attack my bones and spine," Lemieux recalled in his autobiography, *The Final Period.* "I tell you, I did a lot of thinking."

He began skating in early January. His eventual comeback came to symbolize a season in which the Penguins habitually rose from their backs to snatch victory from defeat. They lost Game 1 in each of their four playoff series but rebounded to win the series every time.

WINNERS ABOARD

Prior to the 1990-91 season, general manager Craig Patrick added a couple of veteran Stanley Cup winners to his roster. Plucky winger Joe Mullen came from Calgary, and battle-tested center Bryan Trottier came from the New York Islanders, where he'd won four Cups.

"Badger" Bob Johnson loved Mullen, whom he'd brought to Calgary when Johnson coached the Flames.

Patrick and Johnson sold Trottier on a limited role.

"[Johnson] said, 'I'll use the hell out of you in the playoffs,'" Trottier remembered. "That made the decision real easy."

Still, Trottier had been a franchise player, so he struggled with a bit role.

"There were some tense meetings between Bob and I, but it worked out perfectly. He did play the hell out of me in the playoffs. I was out there in the last minute all the time."

THE TRADE

The Hockey News predicted the Hartford Whalers would win the March 4, 1991 trade in which center Ron Francis and defensemen Ulf Samuelsson and Grant Jennings were shipped to the Penguins for center John Cullen, defenseman Zarley Zalapski, and winger Jeff Parker.

Two months later, the Penguins looked like the winners, because they were the ones parading with the Stanley Cup—thanks largely to Francis and Samuelsson.

Ironically, the Whalers general manager at the time was Eddie Johnston, who'd been the Penguins GM in 1984, when the team drafted Mario Lemieux.

Johnston later said he was under extreme pressure from Whalers management to trade Francis, who'd been stripped of his captaincy.

Penguins general manager Craig Patrick wound up with a future Hall of Famer in Francis and the sort of rugged defenseman the Penguins desperately needed in Samuelsson.

Winless in five games the day of the trade, the Penguins promptly won four in a row and nine of 14 to finish the regular season.

They rolled all the way to their first Stanley Cup. The timing and immediate payoff made it the most dramatic trade in team history.

• • •

Samuelsson endeared himself to the Civic Arena faithful in his very first game, a 4-1 victory over Vancouver. Eventually, fans would chant "Ulf! Ulf! Ulf!" every time he touched the puck.

A city filled with Steelers fans, Pittsburgh loved physical defense.

"So many of the plays I was making before were appreciated by teammates, but never the crowd," Samuelsson said. "To be appreciated for the work you're doing—breaking up plays and hitting—is very special."

At 6-foot-1, 205 pounds, Samuelsson wore a pair of oversized shoulder pads and spent much of his time torturing top forwards such as Boston's Cam Neely. People called Samuelsson a linebacker on skates—and he'd do anything to win a game.

"I'm glad he's on our side," Mario Lemieux said.

Sports Illustrated once did a story on Samuelsson called "Mr. Dirty."

"Even my mother says I'm a dirty player," Samuelsson said.

He finished in the NHL's all-time top 20 in penalty minutes with 2,453.

THE SAVE

"Badger" Bob Johnson had a feeling he'd need back-up goalie Frank Pietrangelo in the 1991 playoffs. That is why he gave Pietrangelo two late-season starts.

But even Johnson couldn't have predicted how big a role Pietrangelo would play in the franchise's first Stanley Cup championship.

The Penguins barely made it out of the first round. They trailed the New Jersey Devils, three games to two, going into Game 6 in New Jersey and were without their best defenseman, Paul Coffey (scratched cornea), and their starting goaltender, Tom Barrasso (bruised shoulder).

Goaltender Wendell Young was injured, too, leaving Bruce Racine—who had never played an NHL game—as Pietrangelo's back up.

Before the game, Johnson told Racine: "No matter what, you're not going in. Don't worry."

Frank Pietrangelo makes "The Save" against New Jersey's Peter Stastny in the '91 playoffs. *(Photo courtesy of the Pittsburgh Penguins)*

The rest of the Penguins had plenty to worry about when New Jersey looked to tie the score 2-2 on a power play late in the first period.

Actually, Penguins equipment manager Steve Latin thought the Devils had tied it when forward Peter Stastny flicked a loose puck toward an open net. Pietrangelo had tried to cover the puck, but John MacLean poked it to Stastny.

"All I did was look up at the scoreboard on the side of the arena and look for them to click it," Latin said.

Several Devils players threw their sticks in the air to celebrate, Pietrangelo noticed as watched the tape later, and Devils fans stood to cheer.

Prematurely, as it turned out.

Pietrangelo lunged to his left and miraculously snagged the puck. It came to be known simply as "The Save" in Pittsburgh hockey lore.

"It was a goal, more or less," Pietrangelo recalled. "It was a bang-bang play, and I made a reaction save. Maybe it gave everyone a lift, like, 'Hey, maybe this is meant to be—maybe we can get it to Game 7.'"

Defenseman Peter Taglianetti was on the ice when it happened. He punched Stastny in the back of the head after the whistle.

"When we went back for a line change, it was like, 'My god, what just happened?'" Taglianetti said. "We knew we dodged a bullet."

The Penguins held on for a 4-3 victory, and Pietrangelo won Game 7, 4-0, before a roaring crowd at the Civic Arena.

Barrasso returned for the next series, but Pietrangelo had carved his place in franchise history. He was doing commercials that summer.

More than a decade later, he became a player agent in Toronto.

"I get asked about the save so many times it's unbelievable," Pietrangelo said. "I'm honored. I really am. And every day I get asked, 'Can I please look at your ring?'"

• • •

Luckily for the Penguins, video replay was not in use during their 1990-91 playoff series against New Jersey. Game 6 of that series is remembered mostly for "The Save," but an equally important near-miss occurred near the end of the second period, when the referee ruled that Devils forward Laurie Boschman kicked the puck into the net. Replays showed that after the puck hit Boschman's skate, it hit his stick, which would have made the goal legal and tied the score going into the third period.

STAR SEARCH

Mario Lemieux, Tom Barrasso, and company weren't the only stars on Civic Arena ice during the early 1990s. A blonde-haired, blue-eyed teenager from Pittsburgh's north suburbs turned heads when she belted out the national anthem on a handful of occasions.

It wasn't until years later, however, that the little girl's name—Christina Aguilera—would be recognized around the world.

BEHIND THE MIKE

Mike Lange's distinctive calls—his first in Pittsburgh was "Great Balls of Fire!"—endeared him to Penguins fans. His calm but entertaining style on television made him a welcome guest in living rooms all over Western Pennsylvania starting in 1979, when Penguins games went from radio, exclusively, to simulcast.

Great Balls of Fire! Mike Lange is inducted into the broadcasters wing of the Hockey Hall of Fame in 2001. *(Photo by James M. Kubus/Pittsburgh Tribune-Review)*

During the Penguins' Stanley Cup years, Lange would exclaim, "Elvis has just left the building!" when a victory was assured (and a fan dressed as Elvis actually would get up and leave the arena at home games).

Lange, a Sacramento, California, native, began with the Penguins in 1974 calling games on radio. He says three of his sayings generated the biggest fan response.

Here's the story behind each:

1. "Scratch my back with a hacksaw" came from a security guard in a Pittsburgh-area shopping mall. "I was going to do a commercial, and I couldn't find the office," Lange said. "He said, 'It's way back in the corner.' Then he said, 'Do you take phrases?' I said, 'Sure.' He wrote it down, and the minute he wrote it down, I thought, 'It's over.' I knew it would work."

2. "He beat him like a rented mule" came from a stockbroker friend. "I called him one day on the phone and asked him how his day went, and he said, 'They're beating me like a rented mule,'" Lange said.

   During a game in the 2003-04 season, Lange altered the call when the Penguins scored a goal against ex-teammate Johan "Moose" Hedberg. Said Lange, "They beat him like a rented Moose!"

3. "Buy Sam a drink and get his dog one, too." Lange overheard this in a bar one night. "A guy walked in and sat down, and that's exactly what he said."

PETER PAN

Defenseman Peter Taglianetti wasn't sure if he could continue playing in a first-round playoff series against the New Jersey Devils in 1991. "Tags" had a case of lace bite, which meant he had a deep bruise in the spot where he flexed his foot and tied his skates.

"Terribly painful," he said.

When word of the problem reached the press, the U.S. and Canadian ski teams offered help. They sent NASA-produced, space-age foam that had worked with skiers' lace bite.

It didn't work with Taglianetti's.

Peanut butter did.

Penguins trainer Skip Thayer remembered a player on the Chicago Blackhawks, Al Secord, using a plastic baggie filled with peanut butter to alleviate lace-bite pain. Secord placed the baggie under the flap of his skate.

Taglianetti tried it and was able to play, which prompted a question: Smooth or crunchy?

"Smooth," he said. "Peter Pan."

When the story reached the papers, a local supermarket chain sent about "10 cases" of peanut butter to the Penguins.

"All the guys took them home to their kids," Taglianetti said.

ROLE PLAYERS

It takes a village to raise a Stanley Cup, which is to say, the Penguins needed everyone on their roster to win championships in 1991 and '92.

There was the so-called Muskegon Line—emergency-recall minor leaguers Jock Callander, Mike Needham, and Dave Michayluk from Muskegon of the International League—and players such as Troy Loney, Frank Pietrangelo, Gordie Roberts, Jiri Hrdina, Jim Paek, Jay Caufield, and Randy Gilhen.

Gilhen scored a huge goal with 4:35 left in regulation of Game 2 of a 1991 second-round series against Washington. It tied the score 6-6, and the Penguins won in overtime.

Afterward, nobody could figure out why Gilhen, a 15-goal scorer, had jumped onto the ice on a delayed penalty with the goalie headed to the bench.

Shouldn't one of the stars have gone?

"Nobody jumped, so I did," Gilhen recalled, laughing. "I went right down the ice, the puck came right to me, and I scored.

"The next day, Badger says to me, 'That was a great goal, but if there's ever a delayed penalty again, I don't want you jumping.'"

CRAZY SKATES

No player was as finicky about his equipment as defenseman Paul Coffey. None wore tighter skates, either.

Coffey, perhaps the smoothest skating defenseman in NHL history, had a shoe size of 9 but wore size 6 skates.

"We had the same shoe size, and I'd put his skates on," equipment manager Steve Latin said. "They used to kill my feet. I couldn't imagine going a whole game like that."

Latin also sharpened Coffey's skates flatter than a tabletop because Coffey didn't do the stopping thing.

"He was always on top of the ice, never sunk in," Latin said. "He just wheeled wherever."

Coffey wheeled his way to more points than any defenseman in Penguins history. He rolled up 440 points in 331 regular-season games and tacked on 26 more in 22 playoff games.

BOLD PREDICTION

The sweat on players' faces hadn't yet dried after Game 2 of the 1991 Stanley Cup semifinals at Boston Garden when Penguins left winger Kevin Stevens made a Joe Namath-like guarantee.

Even though the Penguins trailed, two games to none, and even though the Bruins had been to the Cup final the year before, Stevens guaranteed his team would come back and win the best-of-seven series.

He guaranteed it several times, to anyone within earshot.

"We're like, 'What are you doing? You're throwing fuel on the fire,'" teammate Joe Mullen recalled. "Kevin, being Kevin, was like, 'Don't worry about it.'"

Stevens, a Boston native, was ticked off because the Penguins had dominated the game.

"It was one of those heat-of-the-moment, stupid things I used to say, but I just knew we would beat them," he said. "You just believe in guys."

The Penguins were peeved because Boston scored on a five on three with 3:11 left to tie it, then won on Vladimir Ruzicka's overtime goal.

"I felt we deserved better," Stevens said. "So I said what I said, and people ran with it. The guys got a kick out of it … and it's always nice when it works out."

The Penguins stormed back to win four straight games. After the season, Boston tried to sign Stevens.

"[The guarantee] got me an offer sheet," Stevens said. "[Bruins GM Mike] Milbury thought it was the best thing that ever happened."

HULK HOGAN

Things got ugly in a 1991 Stanley Cup semifinal, when defenseman Ulf Samuelsson knocked Bruins star Cam Neely out of Game 3 with a second-period check.

The next day, Bruins coach Mike Milbury ripped into Penguins coach "Badger" Bob Johnson.

"For all of Bob Johnson's seven-point plans," Milbury said, "there must have been somewhere in that seven-point plan: 'Make sure you take as many cheap shots as you can against the other team's key players.' So the professor of hockey, as he so often projects himself, is also subtly a professor of goonism, and we can't take that any longer."

Johnson's response to Milbury's tirade: "It's confusing, but it's interesting."

Penguins strength and conditioning coach John Welday—a former offensive tackle at Penn State—had a more pointed response.

At the next day's morning skate at the Civic Arena, Welday donned hockey pads and skates. He added a yellow Hulk Hogan tank top, a Hogan head band and boxing gloves and skated onto the ice with a stick in his hands.

You want a goon? You've got one.

Players and reporters howled. Milbury, sitting at the other end of the arena, looked to see what the commotion was about. He then put a newspaper in front of his face and pretended not to notice.

ODD COUPLE

It was an odd pairing, to be sure. Bryan Trottier, a veteran winding down his NHL career, roomed with long-haired, 18-year-old Czech rookie Jaromir Jagr early in the 1990-91 season.

"His English was bad, and my Czechoslovakian was brutal," Trottier said. "All he watched was MTV. He loved Motley Crew and all that. I loved Country Western."

Still, the two formed a bond and wound up playing with Troy Loney on an effective third line.

"We got really, really close," Trottier said.

KEY ASSIST

Mario Lemieux's back was so bad during the Penguins' Stanley Cup drive in 1991 that he could not tie his skates.

Despite crippling back pain, Mario Lemieux managed to score goals like this against Jon Casey in the '91 Stanley Cup Finals. *(Photo courtesy of the Pittsburgh Penguins)*

Lemieux had to sit out Game 3 of the final in Minnesota. Before Game 4, he approached locker-room attendant Tracy Luppe with an unusual request.

"He's like, 'Hey, you have to tie my skates,'" Luppe recalled. "I was like, 'You're the best player in the world; how will I be able to tie your skates?' I said, 'All right, and if you don't like them, I'll re-do 'em.'

"He said, 'Yeah, that's the way it's going to have to be.'"

Luppe laced Lemieux's skates before each game and between each period.

"He could barely move," Luppe said.

Lemieux still won the Conn Smythe Trophy as playoff MVP and managed to score a few spectacular goals.

"I guess I helped out a little bit," Luppe said. "It's my claim to fame, you could say."

Luppe continued to tie Lemieux's skates at the start of the 1991-92 season and again after Lemieux's dramatic comeback from retirement in 2000.

ELECTRIC ATMOSPHERE

"Badger" Bob Johnson called equipment manager Steve Latin into the coaches room before Game 6 of the 1991 Stanley Cup Final at the Met Center in Minneapolis.

The Penguins led the series, three games to two, and were poised to win the first Stanley Cup in their largely calamitous, 24-year history.

Johnson rubbed his face like always and said, "Well, big guy, whaddaya think?"

Replied Latin: "Badger, you could turn the lights off in that dressing room and they'd go right back on, there's so much electricity in there."

Players could not sit still. They'd start to tie their skates and get up to walk around. Kevin Stevens wouldn't stop talking (not that this was anything new).

Mario Lemieux sat in a corner and said nothing.

"It's a pretty good feeling when you're in a locker room and you know you're not going to lose," Stevens said years later. "Every guy had a job to do, and every guy did it. It's fun when you get everybody on the same page. It doesn't happen that often.

"I'll tell you, I miss it. I wish I could go back there."

Ulf Samuelsson opened the scoring, and the Penguins stormed to a 6-0 lead after two periods.

During the second intermission, Latin recalled, some players cried. Latin, as usual, went to notify Johnson that the third period would start in five minutes.

"He was a wreck," Latin said.

Stevens remembered players trying to stay calm. "Even [goalie] Tommy [Barrasso], who said something once in a blue moon, said something. It was pandemonium, then it got quiet, and everybody realized what was going on. It was 6-0. What do you say?"

Only Johnson could find the right words. He picked up a roll of tape and nervously whacked it against a table in the middle of the dressing room, then delivered the expected instructions for the third period—dump the puck, forecheck, don't give up odd-man breaks, etc.

Johnson rarely swore, but before he left the room, he turned to his players and said, "Men, just remember one thing: In 20 minutes, we're going to be world champions. Don't [screw] it up."

Players fought to get through the door. They scored two more goals in the third period en route to an 8-0 victory.

"Nobody would have thought we'd win a Cup," Lemieux said. "But with Bob Johnson, anything's possible."

THINKING OF CULLIE

As the Penguins' first Stanley Cup celebration raged, winger Phil Bourque thought of former teammate John Cullen.

Early in the season, the spirited Cullen was the team's top point producer, helping to make up for the loss of injured star Mario Lemieux. But on March 4, Cullen became a footnote to the Penguins' historical season. He was part of the blockbuster trade that brought Ron Francis and Ulf Samuelsson from the Hartford Whalers.

Bourque was doing a champagne-soaked, dressing room interview with analyst Bill Clement when he made it a point to publicly thank Cullen for his contributions.

"I don't think our team would have been what it was without him," Bourque said. "When Mario went down, Johnny picked his game up so much that he raised everyone else's game. He really carried our team through a very tough time, and he got none of the rewards.

"It's funny that in all that chaos, he was still with me. He should have been there to relish in all that."

LONG, STRANGE TRIP

If the Penguins expected to travel home in luxury the night they won the 1991 Stanley Cup, they were sadly mistaken.

Oh, the flight from Minneapolis to Pittsburgh was fine, but everything that happened thereafter could be filed under the heading, "Comedy of Errors."

The club's travel coordinators were not prepared for the 20,000 fans who crammed the airport and surrounded the team buses—which happened to be school buses on account of a planning glitch.

The players wanted only to get to their cars, but the buses couldn't move amid all the people.

Finally, the bus with the Cup aboard took an alternate route simply to escape the airport. Marketing director Tinsy Labrie was on that bus, along with the likes of Mario Lemieux, Tom Barrasso, Paul Coffey, and Scotty Bowman.

"I remember Tommy Barrasso finally said, 'Let's go to my house and wait it out,'" Labrie said. "So, there we were, sitting on Tom Barrasso's lawn with the Cup on its side as it started to get light out."

It would get more surreal. A few members of the group decided to re-board the bus and head back to the airport to pick up their cars.

The bus ran out of gas on a bridge. Members of the Stanley Cup-winning Pittsburgh Penguins were thus relegated to hitchhiking as the run rose.

"Could this get any more ridiculous?" Labrie wondered.

Soon after, two men on their way to play golf drove by in a pick-up truck and asked if the group needed help. The two men recognized a few of the players.

"They were like, 'Do you want a ride?'" Labrie said. "We took it. I wonder if they still tell that story."

Labrie went into the office that morning to plan for a team celebration in downtown Pittsburgh. One of the first co-workers she saw was Chase Edmondson.

"Chase," she said, "We may be Stanley Cup champions, but we're still the Penguins."

• • •

Broadcaster Mike Lange was in one of the two school buses that carried Penguins personnel after their Stanley Cup victory. The bus had two police escorts—one in front and one behind—followed by legions of cars filled with fans.

Things were moving rather slowly, even as the party aboard progressed rapidly. At one point, Lange remembered, a woman yelled at the driver to stop. She ran off the bus and up a hill to relieve herself in the woods.

"Next thing you know, about 25 guys get off the bus and do the same thing—only we didn't go all the way to the woods," Lange said.

"We're all standing there, in a row, with about a thousand cars waiting."

BITTERSWEET

Even as the Penguins were winning their first Stanley Cup, owner Edward J. DeBartolo was in the midst of selling the team to a group headed by Howard Baldwin.

For people such as team president Paul Martha, a former football star at the University of Pittsburgh, winning the Cup became a bittersweet experience. Martha would not be part of the team's second championship celebration.

"A lot of people with the organization, myself included, didn't understand exactly why it was happening," Martha said. "It had a lot to do with some other businesses the DeBartolos were in."

The purchase price of the Penguins was more than $63 million, the highest price ever paid for an NHL team. Baldwin expressed concern about the team's payroll, which was approaching $11 million, the second highest figure in the NHL.

CUP FOLLIES

Phil Bourque decided that Mario Lemieux's pool party wasn't lively enough. The Penguins had won the 1991 Stanley Cup a few days earlier, and Lemieux's pool, it should be noted, featured a waterfall lit with neon lights.

"I was sitting in the hot tub with the wives and girlfriends and I go, 'You know what? It's time to get this party started,'" Bourque recalled. "I hiked up the waterfall in my underwear and put the Cup over my head, like King Kong on top of the Empire State Building.

"No disrespect to the Cup or anything, but I heaved it into the swimming pool. There are a whole bunch of pictures out there of it actually in mid-air."

"It wasn't a great idea," said teammate Bob Errey.

The Cup, of course, is hollow. It immediately filled with water and sunk to the bottom of the pool. Bourque dived to retrieve it but had to come up and ask for help.

"It took about four of us to bring the thing up," he said. "But as soon as it went down there, everybody started jumping in the pool, and that's when the party got hopping."

The real party occurred the next day in downtown Pittsburgh, where it seemed as if the entire city came out to celebrate the Penguins' first title.

And if the players were in bad shape that morning, they had nothing on the Cup.

"I understand they needed a silversmith to polish it up that morning, because all the chlorine had tarnished it," Bourque said. "It was kind of a rust brown color."

Worse, the top of the Cup was loose. That is why pictures of that day's celebration show players holding it from the bottom and sides in front of 40,000 fans at Point State Park.

"The bowl was loose, and there was a sign inside the bowl," Errey said. "It said, 'Don't Grab Top of Cup.'"

ROSE GARDEN

On June 24, 1991, the Stanley Cup-champion Penguins became the first NHL team to visit the White House, where president George Bush greeted them.

Thrilled to be there, the players were not insulted when the President said, "And you are?" as Mario Lemieux stepped forward.

"He wasn't a hockey fan," defenseman Larry Murphy said, "and I don't think he was trying to pass himself off as one."

TRAGIC NEWS

As the Penguins celebrated on a bus ride back from the airport after winning their first Stanley Cup, one man was uncharacteristically quiet.

"I remember Badger Bob just sat in the front of the bus," broadcaster Mike Lange said. "He was just not himself."

Johnson, as it turned out, was gravely ill.

Three months later, on August 29, 1991, Martha Johnson had her husband taken to Pittsburgh's Mercy Hospital with stroke-like symptoms. Emergency surgery was performed to remove a tumor, but an inoperable one remained.

"Badger" Bob Johnson had brain cancer. It progressed quickly. He died on November 26, squeezing every last minute out of his life. At the depth of his illness, he was helping his Team USA squad to a silver-medal finish at the Canada Cup by mapping out strategy from his hospital bed.

Penguins fans and players kept "Badger Bob" close to their hearts during the second Stanley Cup run. *(Photo courtesy of the Pittsburgh Penguins)*

The Penguins visited Johnson during a preseason trip to Denver. Unable to speak, he wore a Penguins T-shirt and wrote notes to his players.

"We all had an opportunity to look in his eyes for the last time," center Bryan Trottier recalled. "He was such a big part of our success, a big part of the change in the atmosphere of the Penguins organization. His favorite saying said it all: 'It's a great day for hockey.'"

● ● ●

The night after Johnson's death, Penguins fans paid tribute to him before a Thanksgiving Eve game against New Jersey.

Fans were given battery-powered candles, the Civic Arena ice was inscribed with a message that read, "It's A Great Day For Hockey— Badger Bob," and the arena was darkened as Karla Bonoff sang "Goodbye, My Friend."

"I'll always remember that night, with the lights out and the candles lit," winger Joe Mullen said. "I knew hockey was going to miss Badger very much."

The Penguins scored four of the night's final five goals to win handily. Six days later, coaches, players, wives, and front-office workers flew to Colorado Springs, on the team's way to Edmonton, for Badger Bob's funeral.

Equipment manager Steve Latin keeps one of Johnson's ever-present notebooks, in which Johnson would scribble endlessly.

"I'll open it up when times are rough," Latin said. "When we had that 18-game winless streak [midway through the 2003-04 season], I opened it up and felt better right away."

Considering the impact Johnson had, it's amazing Pittsburgh knew him for only 17 months.

TOCCHET TRADE

In February of 1992, general manager Craig Patrick was set to make his second blockbuster trade in as many years. He was hoping it would propel the Penguins to a Stanley Cup, the way his deal with the Hartford Whalers had the year before.

This time, Patrick wanted to send popular winger Mark Recchi to the Philadelphia Flyers as part of a package that would reel in power forward Rick Tocchet, hulking defenseman Kjell Samuelsson, and veteran goalie Ken Wregget.

Patrick called a meeting that included coach Scotty Bowman and assistant coaches Barry Smith, Rick Kehoe, and Pierre McGuire. He asked everyone to vote on the deal.

Bowman was the only one who voted against it, afraid Recchi would outdo Tocchet.

Patrick made the trade anyway, and Bowman soon realized that Tocchet provided an element of toughness the Penguins needed, not to mention an excellent scoring touch.

Both were displayed on March 15 at Chicago, shortly after the trade, when Tocchet scored two third-period goals wearing a football-style helmet. He'd left the game in the second period because of a broken jaw.

The Penguins would meet the Blackhawks again in the Stanley Cup final.

"Scotty became a huge Rick Tocchet fan," McGuire recalled. "He realized we needed Tocchet if we were going to beat Chicago in Chicago in the finals."

GOALIES CHANGE ON THE FLY

Always creative coach Scotty Bowman hatched one of his more interesting ideas on April 16, 1992, the final day of the regular season: He planned to switch goalies Ken Wregget and Wendell Young every five minutes in a meaningless game at Madison Square Garden against the Rangers.

Apparently, a team from some other era had won a Cup after using the same strategy in its final regular-season game.

Young thought it was a crazy idea, but he was willing to take it one step further, without telling Bowman.

As long as we're going to change so often, Young figured, why not change on the fly?

"I told the guys, 'Throw some money in, and we'll do it,'" Young recalled. "They were like, 'No way you're going to do that.' I said, 'I will. I don't care, and you know what? We'll do a high-five and low-five when we change, and I'm going to moon walk back to the crease.'"

Wregget recalled the pot rising to about $400. He started the game, and sure enough, five minutes later, Young jumped over the boards.

Wregget skated off, and the two managed a weak high-five but had no time for further shenanigans, because Mark Messier was leading a three-on-one break for the Rangers.

"I was like, 'Oh my god,'" Young said.

Wregget's pads caught on top of the boards, and he toppled over. The Rangers didn't score. Not that time, anyway. The Penguins lost, 7-1.

Young and Wregget wondered if Bowman would be mad. He was thrilled.

"Scotty loved it, because he always wanted to be part of something new," Young said. "Somebody said to him, 'Those guys didn't change on the fly,' and he said, 'Yes, they did. Yes they did.'

"He wanted to be the coach [who was a] part of goalies changing on the fly."

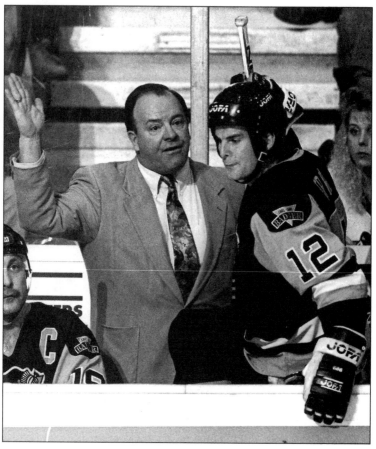

Enigmatic coach Scotty Bowman sends Bob Errey over the boards in 1991-92.
(Photo courtesy of the Pittsburgh Penguins)

CLOSED-DOOR MEETING

Eddie Johnston, then Hartford Whalers general manager, was supposed to be the Penguins coach for the 1992-93 season, but the teams could not work out a salary agreement, so Scotty Bowman was retained.

Bowman's return was announced the morning of the team's October 6 opener against Philadelphia and did not produce cheers in the dressing room.

Players weren't thrilled with the way Bowman ran practices (something he didn't do in the final part his two-year tenure with the Penguins). They would half-jokingly ask equipment manager Steve Latin to hide Bowman's skates and once stuffed cotton in the airhorn Bowman used to signal line changes.

Late in Bowman's first season behind the bench—1991-92 —the issue came to a head during a meeting March 2 at the team hotel in Calgary.

There were no coaches present, just general manager Craig Patrick and the players. Patrick called the gathering. The team had won only two of its previous 12 games and was threatening to become the first Stanley Cup champion in 22 years to miss the playoffs.

Everybody sat in a small ballroom.

"Our team was just in disarray," winger Phil Bourque recalled.

After a few players spouted clichés about working harder and the like, Bourque, Peter Taglianetti, and Bob Errey, among others, spoke up.

"I flat-out said to Craig, 'I don't think we can win with Scotty Bowman,'" Bourque recalled. "Everybody kind of scooched back in their seats like holy [cow], what the heck is he doing?"

Patrick did not say much. He sat and listened as other players chimed in with their thoughts.

According to Bourque, Patrick said, "Scotty is very different, but he is the winningest coach in hockey, and there's a reason why. Maybe you don't understand it now. I agree with everything everybody's saying, except for what [Bourque] said. I think we can win with Scotty Bowman, and we will win with Scotty Bowman."

Patrick subsequently spoke with Bowman, and the situation improved.

"We each took a step toward each other," Bourque said. "From there, it was a different hockey team."

STRANGE LINE

Nobody could believe it when Scotty Bowman wrote out his lines on the chalkboard before Game 1 of a 1992 playoff series against the Washington Capitals.

Mario Lemieux was injured, so Bowman put checker Troy Loney between high scorers Kevin Stevens and Rick Tocchet.

"Everybody was kind of looking at me, and I was like, 'What?'" Loney said. "Scotty never asked me if I'd played center before—which

I hadn't—he just threw me in there, which was typical of the way he could keep you off balance.

"Well, I think Tocchet and Stevens were sour as hell, but I was having a great time."

The experiment lasted approximately 10 minutes.

GRAVES ATTACK

New York Rangers forward Adam Graves became a marked man in Pittsburgh during a 1992 playoff series, when his wicked, baseball-swing slash broke Mario Lemieux's left hand at 5:05 of the second period of Game 2.

Lemieux was finished for the series and was not expected back in the playoffs. The NHL suspended Graves for four games, but only after he scored in a 6-5 victory in Game 3 that gave the Rangers a 2-1 lead in the best-of-seven series.

Graves' comment: "Obviously, you have to be more cautious in the way you're checking a guy."

Adam Graves became enemy No. 1 in Pittsburgh when he broke Mario Lemieux's wrist with a wicked slash in the '92 playoffs. *(Photo by James M. Kubus/Pittsburgh Tribune-Review)*

Lemieux ripped the NHL as "too dangerous" and said he felt the Roger Neilson-led Rangers had put out "a contract" on him.

The incident sparked the Penguins, who roared back from a 4-2 deficit midway through the third period to win Game 4, 6-5 in overtime.

Ron Francis started the rally when he beat Mike Richter from behind the blue line, just after a five-minute major against the Penguins had expired.

"I was just looking to get off the ice," Francis recalled.

The shot caromed in off Richter's glove.

"You can't give them an inch," Richter told reporters. "But that's what I gave them: an inch."

The Penguins took a mile. Jaromir Jagr stole Game 5 with a spectacular performance, including a penalty-shot goal.

Lemieux returned in the following series against Boston with a small cast on his left hand. In order to allow him to grip his sticks, the training staff shaved the tops of them as thin as a putter.

• • •

When Francis arrived home after scoring a hat trick in Game 4, he found a few hats hanging from a small tree in his yard. His next-door neighbor had put them there.

"The next morning, there had to be about 25 hats on that tree," Francis said. "It was pretty funny."

PIECE OF ART

Mario Lemieux put the perfect finishing touch on the Penguins' playoff sweep of the Boston Bruins in 1992.

The Penguins were short-handed late in Game 4, leading 4-1, when Lemieux knocked the puck out of mid-air and headed down the ice against future Hall of Fame defenseman Raymond Bourque. Penguins players stood on the bench to watch what would become one of the great goals in team annals.

Lemieux tortured Bourque, throwing the puck at his feet so that Bourque could not turn around.

Finally, Lemieux grabbed the puck with a dramatic swoop and roofed a shot over goaltender Andy Moog's left shoulder from about two feet out.

"It was an amazing thing," said Penguins winger Kevin Stevens.

Bruins coach Rick Bowness called the goal "a piece of art."

Bourque, of course, was the same man Lemieux had victimized on his first NHL goal, eight years earlier.

SETTING A TRAP

The Penguins of the early 1990s are remembered as a free-wheeling, offensive juggernaut, but they wouldn't have won their second Stanley Cup if they hadn't dropped into a passive, 1-4 trap against the Washington Capitals in a second-round series.

Washington had built a three-games-to-one lead by capitalizing on Penguins turnovers and by springing their active and talented defense into the rush.

Basically, the Capitals were waiting for the overaggressive Penguins to mess up.

A day before Game 5, the Penguins decided they could play the waiting game, too. Mario Lemieux and Ron Francis approached coach Scotty Bowman with the idea of playing a 1-4 system that would clog the neutral zone.

"I was in the training room," recalled forward Bryan Trottier. "Mario and Ronnie were talking about how Washington was counteracting our forecheck. They said we could clog everything at the blue line, not be as aggressive and go into a 1-4. In our end, if the Capitals dumped it in, [goaltender] Tommy [Barrasso] could play the puck so well, he could just fire it out on his forehand.

"I don't remember Scotty being all that enthusiastic about it, but when you're down 1-3, you're willing to give it a shot."

The strategy achieved swift and stunning results.

"It changed the series right around," winger Joe Mullen said.

The Penguins grabbed a 3-0 lead in Game 5 and won the final three games by a combined score of 14-7.

THE SLIDE

It was softspoken general manager Craig Patrick, of all people, who sparked a chain of events that led to Bryan Trottier's memorable slide at a 1992 Stanley Cup celebration.

The 40,000 fans who filled Three Rivers Stadium that day were growing a bit restless in the drizzle.

Bryan Trottier takes his memorable slide on the rain-covered tarp at Three Rivers Stadium. *(Photo courtesy of the Pittsburgh Penguins)*

"We were waiting for the mayor or something," Trottier said. "Well, Craig comes up to me and goes, 'We better do something to get the crowd going. Grab the Cup and do something.'"

Trottier asked a group of teammates to join him in a romp around the stadium. They agreed but left him out to dry when he stepped off the podium.

"I took four steps away, and all those guys were grinning, those creeps," Trottier said. "Now, I'm feeling a little conspicuous. At the same time, I said, 'I'm committed.'"

Trottier saw that the infield tarp looked mighty slick. Without a second thought, he took a running start and slid on his back, the Cup clenched in his hands.

The splashy slide seemed as if it would never end. The crowd went wild.

"Craig slapped me on the back and said, 'That was great,'" Trottier said. "It turned out to be something a lot of people remember. I'll bump into people at airports, malls, wherever, and they say, 'That was awesome.'"

STANLEY HEADS TO THE HOSPITAL

The Penguins arrived home from Chicago in the wee hours of the morning after winning their second straight Stanley Cup in 1992. The equipment men and trainers were showering when locker-room attendant Tracy Luppe announced he was going to take the Cup for a little spin.

Jaromir Jagr and Mario Lemieux celebrate their second consecutive Stanley Cup victory. *(Photo courtesy of the Pittsburgh Penguins)*

Luppe's girlfriend worked at West Penn Hospital, so he loaded the Cup onto the back of his truck and drove it there for a visit.

It had only been 10 hours since the end of the game.

"I stunk like champagne and everything, and when I got on the elevator at the hospital, everybody was like, 'Oh my God, that's the Stanley Cup,'" Luppe recalled.

He walked into the labor and delivery department, where his girlfriend worked, and said, "Here's the Stanley Cup. I need some sleep."

Luppe grabbed a power nap in a delivery room, while the rest of the floor went nuts. Newborns were photographed in the Cup. Adults were photographed next to it.

"No way was anybody getting any help at the time," Luppe said. "When I woke up, you couldn't move, there were so many people on the floor."

LIFE'S A BEACH

Jaromir Jagr made quite a stir in Pittsburgh after delivering a memorable quote to *Sports Illustrated* in the summer of 1992. The team had just won its second consecutive Stanley Cup, but money problems were rearing their ugly head. The Penguins had a long history of such problems.

The future held a few, as well.

"If they have no money, I want to be traded where there's beaches," Jagr said. "I have two Stanley Cup rings. I don't need more rings. I just need money and beaches and girls."

Jagr never did get another ring. He was traded in the summer of 2001.

GARAGE LEAGUE

On January 26, 1992, Mario Lemieux tore into the NHL after a 6-4 loss at Washington, in which the Capitals had basically mugged the faster, more talented Penguins.

Jaromir Jagr was so frustrated that he knocked referee Ron Hoggarth to his knees during the game.

Afterward, Lemieux fired off a memorable scolding.

"It's a skating and passing game—that's what the fans want to see," he said. "The advantage is to the marginal player now. That's the way this garage league is run."

Commissioner John Ziegler fined Lemieux $1,000.

MIRACLE MAN

Philadelphia sports fans once booed Santa Claus, but they couldn't help but cheer Mario Lemieux on March 2, 1993, when he performed perhaps the most dramatic feat of his career.

Fewer than 12 hours before the puck dropped, Lemieux was undergoing the last of his radiation treatments for Hodgkin's disease.

Soon after, he boarded a plane to Philadelphia. Fans gave him a 90-second ovation when he appeared on the ice for the national anthem.

Coach Scotty Bowman planned to play Lemieux limited minutes, but that went out the window in the first period.

"We didn't think he was ready yet, but that's Mario," winger Joe Mullen said. "He played a great game that night, too."

Lemieux finished with a goal and an assist in a 5-4 loss.

"I wanted to come back earlier," he told reporters. "But the doctors wouldn't let me."

● ● ●

When he returned from his treatments for Hodgkin's disease, Lemieux trailed Buffalo's Pat LaFontaine by 12 points in the NHL scoring race. The deficit shrank quickly. Lemieux racked up 30 goals and 56 points in the final 20 games to finish with 160 points. He won the scoring title by 12 points.

"I thought about it even during radiation," Lemieux said. "I was determined to come back and regain the lead."

UGLY INCIDENT

Former television analyst Paul Steigerwald recalled a horrific night in 1993, when play-by-play man Mike Lange was attacked on the street in Toronto.

"I had just returned to the hotel from the morning skate, when Mike called and asked me to come to his room. I knocked on the door, and he stood behind it as he invited me in," Steigerwald said. "When I stepped into the room, I was horrified by the sight of this almost unrecognizable apparition. His face was literally four times its normal size, and his lips were the size of hot dogs. I am not exaggerating when I say he looked an awful lot like the 'Elephant Man.'"

Lange proceeded to tell his partner what happened the night before. Some nutcase apparently ran up and sucker-punched Lange in the jaw as Lange munched a slice of pizza. He spent most of the night in the hospital having his teeth repaired.

Steigerwald thought Lange was going to ask him to handle the play by play that night, but Lange explained that he wanted Steigerwald to be on camera by myself to open the telecast, then toss it to Lange off-camera for the faceoff.

"His speech was slightly garbled, and he spoke rather economically, but he was otherwise on top of his game," Steigerwald said. "It has to be considered one the most incredible performances in the history of sports broadcasting—and it was typical of Mike's unflappable belief that the show must go on. It should not surprise you to know that he never has missed a broadcast because of illness in all his years with the Penguins."

BLUE FEET

Somehow, somebody got their hands on the fine powder that authorities use to snag bank robbers. It's the kind of stuff that turns blue on the skin when a person sweats.

Well somebody put it in assistant coach Rick Paterson's socks before practice one day.

After the workout, equipment manager Steve Latin heard screams coming from the coaches room.

"I look, and Rick is standing there completely naked," Latin said. "But from his ankles down, he was all blue. I don't know which player did that."

Paterson, no doubt, made every effort to find out.

ALL-STAR PENGUINS

Mike Ramsey had seen a lot in his hockey career. Heck, he'd been a member of the 1980 U.S. Olympic team that performed the miracle on ice.

But he couldn't believe his eyes when he walked into the Penguins dressing room on March 22, 1993, the day the Penguins acquired him from the Buffalo Sabres in exchange for Bob Errey.

The Penguins had recently launched what would become an NHL-record, 17-game winning streak. The team boasted the likes of

Mario Lemieux, Ron Francis, Tom Barrasso, Jaromir Jagr, Rick Tocchet, Joe Mullen, Kevin Stevens, and Larry Murphy.

Ramsey's reaction: "I thought I was at the All-Star Game."

AT WHAT COST?

Most would agree that the 1992-93 Penguins, with four 100-point scorers, were the best team in franchise history.

"By far," left winger Kevin Stevens said. "We were a machine."

Certainly, they were heavy favorites to win a third consecutive Stanley Cup after finishing the season with an NHL-record 17-game winning streak (and a tie in the season finale).

The Penguins knew they were on a roll when defenseman Ulf Samuelsson—who had 11 goals in 277 games with the team—beat Montreal's Patrick Roy in overtime on April 7, giving the team its 15th consecutive victory. That tied the New York Islanders' league record.

But the winning streak, as it turned out, might have spent valuable energy reserves that would have come in handy in a second-round playoff series against—who else?—the Islanders.

Players such as Ron Francis have said the team became consumed with the streak, to the point where it might have been a distraction, or perhaps bred overconfidence.

"We were winning; the problem was, we weren't playing well," defenseman Larry Murphy said. "We were just kind of fluking our way through the whole thing. Once we got into the playoffs, we didn't handle adversity too well."

The Islanders eliminated the Penguins in seven games. Stevens doesn't believe the streak affected his team negatively.

"The Islanders always gave us fits," he said. "We had one tough series every year, and it was going to be that series that year. We had to find a way to get by them, and we didn't. We could've beaten the rest of those teams skating backwards."

HORRIFIC INJURY

Kevin Stevens wanted to hit New York Islanders defenseman Rich Pilon something fierce. It was early in the first period of the seventh game of a second-round playoff series in 1993.

"He was playing on me the whole series, driving me crazy," Stevens recalled. "We had 10 years of history, too. I just went to hit him, and

Kevin Stevens was a powerful force in both of the Penguins' Stanley Cup seasons.
(Photo courtesy of the Pittsburgh Penguins)

I really hit him. But he had his shield on, and he leads with his head, and I got knocked out."

In mid-air, no less.

Stevens landed face-first with a sickening thud. He sustained a broken nose and a fractured frontal sinus bone. The injury required several hours of reconstructive surgery.

The way Stevens sees it, the Penguins might have avoided a stunning 4-3 loss to the underdog Islanders if not for the incident.

"I think I could have made a difference somewhere in there."

CRUSHING BLOW

The name David Volek is enough to turn stomachs all over Pittsburgh.

Volek's goal at 5:16 of overtime in Game 7 of a 1993 second-round playoff series stunned a Civic Arena crowd and gave the upstart New York Islanders a 4-3 victory.

The best team in Penguins history was finished. A potential dynasty was ruined.

This was the third time the Islanders eliminated the Penguins in the deciding game of a playoff series.

A rugged young defenseman named Darius Kasparaitis—who would later join the Penguins—tortured Jaromir Jagr and Mario Lemieux, and Islanders coach Al Arbour made all the right moves.

"It was one of Al's greatest coaching jobs, shuffling lines and matching personnel," said former Islanders GM Bill Torrey.

The Islanders played the series without their best player, Pierre Turgeon.

"Without a doubt, we should have won it," said Penguins defenseman Larry Murphy. "It just goes to show: The best team doesn't always win the Stanley Cup."

Lemieux would later say that he'd run out of gas by playoff time. Understandably so, considering he spent part of the season battling Hodgkin's disease.

MARATHON GAME

As much as the Islanders tormented the Penguins, so the Penguins tormented the Washington Capitals.

Never more so than on April 24, 1996, at USAir Arena, when the Penguins won Game 4 of a first-round playoff series, 3-2, at precisely 79:15 of overtime.

In other words, the teams played a doubleheader and then some. It was the third longest game in NHL history and the longest in six decades.

Petr Nedved's winning goal occurred six hours, 37 minutes after the opening faceoff, as Mario Lemieux and Tom Barrasso watched on television.

Barrasso left the game with back spasms at the start of the second period. Lemieux had been tossed out in the second period for attacking Todd Krygier, who had dumped Lemieux to the ice without a penalty (Lemieux later joked that he should be able to rejoin the action, seeing as he'd sat out the equivalent of a full game).

Among the other sidelights:

- Penguins coach Eddie Johnston was hit by a puck on the bench, opening a gash on his head that required 18 stitches to close.
- Penguins goalie Ken Wregget stopped the first overtime penalty shot in playoff history (Joe Juneau) and made 53 saves.
- Capitals rookie Olaf Kolzig made 62 saves.
- Fans without tickets showed up at the rink during the overtimes, walked in for free and watched.

Nedved finally won it on the power play with 44.6 seconds left in the fourth overtime. He took a pass from Sergei Zubov and fired a turnaround wrist shot from the left circle that sailed through a crowd and over Kolzig's left shoulder.

"It was getting to the point," Nedved said, "where I didn't really think anybody was going to score."

WEIGHT OF THE WORLD

Mario Lemieux's wife, Nathalie, endured a difficult pregnancy with the couple's first son. It kept her husband on edge for weeks, although his struggle was only known among the Penguins' inner circle.

When Austin Lemieux finally arrived in a premature birth, his father was highly relieved—and greatly inspired.

He was ready to play hockey again. The St. Louis Blues were next on the schedule, and it just happened to be Wayne Gretzky's first (and last) game in Pittsburgh as a member of the St. Louis Blues.

March 26, 1996.

Lemieux ranks the game among his best hockey memories. He finished with five goals and eight points in an 8-4 victory. It tied the single-best performance of his career.

On his final goal of the night, Lemieux took a pass from Ron Francis, beat goalie Jon Casey and finally came to rest on his back against the end boards, where he lay on the ice with a giddy smile—as if he had amazed even himself.

ONE-PUNCH KNOCKOUT

Maybe it was the boxing lessons Chris Tamer took as a teen. Whatever the case, he delivered one of the more dramatic punches in Penguins history when he felled Chicago Blackhawks heavyweight Bob Probert with a short left during Tamer's rookie season in 1996.

Tamer never became a noted NHL fighter, but that punch gave him a lasting reputation.

"I guess he didn't see that left coming," Tamer later said. "He was facing my left side and obviously didn't have a tight grip on it. I don't get a great deal of satisfaction from that. I give myself credit for just showing up for the fight."

FAREWELL, MARIO

Few expected the Penguins to win the Stanley Cup in 1997. They'd blown a golden chance the year before, losing to the underdog Florida Panthers in the Eastern Conference final.

To add to the gloom, Mario Lemieux left little doubt that the 1996-97 season would be his last. He confirmed as much in early April, and it seemed as if he would go out quietly.

The Penguins trailed the Philadelphia Flyers in a first-round series, three games to none, going into Game 4 at the Civic Arena.

Mustering some untapped heart, the Penguins jumped on the Flyers early and were ahead 3-1 as the clock started to wind down.

Fans began chanting Lemieux's name—"Mar-ee-oh! Mar-ee-oh!"—midway through the third period. Everyone realized this could be his last game in Pittsburgh, because the series was shifting to Philadelphia for Game 5.

Could Le Magnifique possibly produce one last piece of drama? Of course he could.

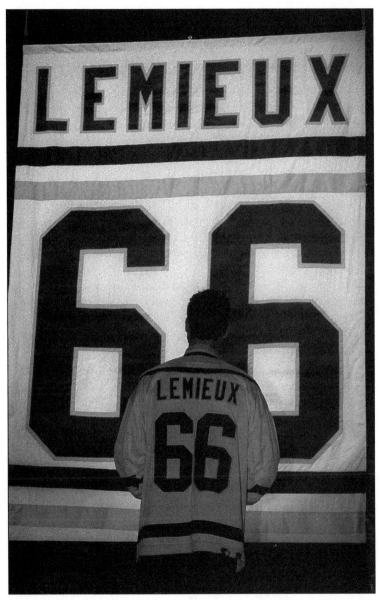

Little did anyone know that when Mario Lemieux's jersey was raised to the rafters in 1997, it would be lowered three years later. *(Photo by James M. Kubus/Pittsburgh Tribune-Review)*

With 1:04 left, he took a pass from Ian Moran and skated in on a breakaway against goalie Garth Snow. The building seemed to hold its breath.

It exploded in cheers when Lemieux scored a picture-perfect goal. He promptly looked to the heavens with his hands outstretched, palms up, as if to offer thanks.

"It was perfect," said the Penguins' Craig Patrick, who was interim coach at the time. "Couldn't write a better script than that."

The normally stoic Lemieux, just 31 at the time, played the final seconds with tears welling in his eyes (the Penguins lost the next game).

"It's the first time I've cried after a game," he said. "It's something I'll always remember."

The rest of Pittsburgh cried with him, realizing that one of the great athletes of the 20th century was never to perform in front of them again.

Or so they thought.

5

HIGHS AND LOWS

(1997-2004)

WHAT A DRAG

Star right winger Jaromir Jagr got himself into plenty of hot water in the summer of 1999, when the Czech tabloid *Blesk* ran a story in which he was quoted as saying the difference between his native Czech Republic and Pittsburgh was like the difference "between heaven and hell."

Jagr insisted he'd been misquoted, just as he had a few months earlier when a Czech newspaper quoted him ripping Penguins coach Kevin Constantine.

It just so happened that when the *Blesk* story came out, Jagr was photographed dressed in drag for a charity function in the Czech Republic. He wore a red wig, blush and lipstick to go with a flowery dress.

The *Hockey News* ran both stories with a brilliant headline: "Miss Quote."

JAYWALKER

A simple search for a dinner spot turned into a fiasco one night in Calgary when long-haired, Lithuanian defenseman Darius Kasparaitis was cited for jaywalking.

Kasparaitis was ordered into the back of a squad car. He refused. He waited for teammates Brad Werenka, Hans Jonsson, and Rob Brown to catch up.

Jaromir Jagr as "Miss Quote." *(Photo by Ales Krecl/AFP)*

After the players piled into the back seat, Kasparaitis proceeded to tell the officer that Werenka was from Mexico. The officer threatened to kick Kasparaitis out of the country, which would have put a crimp in his plans to play the following night.

"The cop started getting a sense of humor after talking to Kaspar for about 15 minutes," Werenka said. "He lightened up and drove us to a restaurant."

Eventually, Kasparaitis offered the cop tickets to the next night's game. Brown recalled that by the end of the ride, the players were laughing so hard they were crying.

"Only Kaspar could cause these kinds of problems," Brown said. "He could have been the first Lithuanian kicked out of Canada."

WANNA FIGHT?

When a 55-year-old Florida Panthers fan named Keith Hubbell made fun of Matthew Barnaby's injured eye, he had no idea Barnaby would take such offense.

Obviously, he didn't know Barnaby very well.

The incident occurred moments after Barnaby held on for dear life in an altercation with towering Panthers enforcer Peter Worrell. As Barnaby left the ice and headed down the runway to the dressing room, Hubbell, seated next to the Penguins' bench, yelled to him, 'How many fingers do I have up?'"

Barnaby turned around and raced toward Hubbell. He reached into the stands and grabbed Hubbell's arm. Hubbell then cocked his fists as if he was ready to fight.

He was glad he didn't.

"You would be talking to a dead man," he said.

Barnaby was suspended for four games, forfeiting $53,658.54 of his $1.1 million salary.

HAIRY SITUATION

Training camp wasn't 10 minutes old in 1999 when word began to spread about the biggest cut in Penguins history.

Jaromir Jagr's hair was gone.

Most of it, anyway. Jagr's trademark curly locks were strewn on a barbershop floor in Rome.

"I was in Italy and told them to make me look like an Italian," Jagr told reporters. "They have short hair like this. ... I think I'm old enough to have short hair now."

Jagr's teammates were astounded to see that their captain, who once could have passed for a rock star, now looked like a linebacker for the University of Pittsburgh's football team.

"I had to introduce myself to him," teammate Tyler Wright said.

GOAL JUDGE

On September 3, 1999, inside a federal courtroom at the USX Tower in downtown Pittsburgh, U.S. Bankruptcy Judge Bernard J. Markovitz pulled off one of the great plays in Penguins history.

Markovitz weaved through 10 months of red tape and political haggling to set up Mario Lemieux for a tap-in goal.

In authorizing Lemieux's plan to buy the franchise out of bankruptcy, Markovitz likely prevented the NHL from disbanding the team, or perhaps relocating it to a city such as Portland, Oregon.

The Penguins had been $100 million in debt when they filed for bankruptcy the previous October.

Lemieux said goodbye to more than $20 million owed to him on his final contract and took a $25 million equity stake in the team. He defeated Civic Arena operator SMG and Fox Sports Pittsburgh, who banded together in an attempt to outbid him.

The Penguins had spent nearly a year snared in tumultuous bankruptcy proceedings. Markovitz needed less than a half-hour to settle the matter.

The judge looked up from his chair and said, "All right, this is done. Now the puck is on Mr. Lemieux's stick, and we've all seen what he's been able to do with that."

The Penguins broke even in their first four seasons under Lemieux's ownership.

ALL IN A NAME

On December 20, 1999, the 38-year-old Civic Arena became Mellon Arena, as financial giant Mellon Financial Corp. paid $18 million for a 10-year naming-rights deal.

"Life begins at 40 for the Mellon Arena," said Tom Rooney, the Penguins' chief operating officer.

A name change almost occurred two years earlier, when Allegheny Energy Inc. and the Penguins announced a deal whereby the building would be called the Allegheny Energy Dome.

The deal fell through because the Penguins, then co-owned by Howard Baldwin, failed to tell the Public Auditorium Authority about the offer. The Public Auditorium Authority owned the arena.

WORLD BEATERS

The Penguins took center stage when the Czech Republic stunned the world by winning an Olympic gold medal in 1998 in Nagano, Japan.

Four Penguins—Jaromir Jagr, Robert Lang, Martin Straka and Jiri Slegr—were key members of the Czech team. They took part in a wild celebration in Prague's Old Town Square, where more than 130,000 adoring fans came to cheer, then boarded a plane for Montreal.

Though bleary-eyed from more than 30 hours of travel over the previous three days, they led the way in a 6-2 victory over the Canadiens.

Lang scored 52 seconds into the game. Jagr had four points.

All four players will forever remember the party in Prague.

"When we came off the plane and I saw all the people, I started crying," Straka said. "My dream came true."

"We were not playing for ourselves," Jagr told the crowd. "We were playing for 10 million people."

HEARD 'ROUND THE LEAGUE

This must have been what the Coliseum in ancient Rome sounded like. Penguins fans cheered maniacally on March 7, 1998, as Philadelphia Flyers star Eric Lindros crawled along the ice, desperately trying to regain his senses.

Seconds earlier, Lindros had absorbed a knockout hit from Penguins defenseman Darius Kasparaitis. The Penguins trailed 4-3 with 11:12 left in the second period. Momentum quickly turned.

Lindros sustained a concussion—one of many that would eventually threaten his career—and stayed overnight at a Pittsburgh hospital.

The Penguins won, 6-4, but the same two teams were scheduled to play the next night in Philadelphia. Kasparaitis might as well have had his face plastered on a most-wanted sign.

Darius Kasparaitis left an indelible mark on Penguins history.
(Photo courtesy of the Pittsburgh Penguins)

A little more than three minutes into the game, Dainius Zubrus and Rod Brind'Amour tried to gang-tackle Kasparaitis. After the Flyers scored a power-play goal, they went after him again.

Brind'Amour drilled him, then Colin Forbes pounded him behind the Penguins' net.

"I knew they were going to come after me," Kasparaitis said, flashing his mischievous smile. "I just had to be careful."

GREAT GOAL

Jaromir Jagr had a knack for scoring dramatic and spectacular goals. Few, if any, were more spectacular than the one he scored on March 13, 1999, in a home game against the Philadelphia Flyers.

Flyers defenseman Luke Richardson pulled Jagr to the ice on the play, but Jagr still managed to release a weak backhander. The puck deflected off goalie Ron Hextall's blocker, and Jagr, sliding on his stomach, reached up and flicked it under the crossbar for his 32nd goal and 100th point of the season.

"We're witnessing something that's going to be on the highlight reel forever, regarding one of the greatest goals ever scored," Penguins coach Kevin Constantine said.

Jagr called the goal "an accident."

Others knew better.

"Maybe it was lucky," teammate Martin Straka said. "But it's the great players who get lucky all the time."

NOWHERE TO BE FOUND

When the Penguins started 8-14-3 under Kevin Constantine in 1999-2000, general manager Craig Patrick decided it was time for a change.

Constantine had presided over the best defensive team in Penguins history—and the only division winner between 1996-2004—two seasons earlier, but his relationship with Jagr had soured. The team had gone south.

Patrick called on old friend, Herb Brooks, who was scouting for the Penguins. Patrick had been Brooks' assistant coach with the U.S. Olympic team in 1980 and was convinced that Brooks could help turn the team around, if only he could be found.

Brooks, near his home in Minnesota, was getting his transmission fluid changed at the time.

When the Penguins faltered early in the 1999-2000 season, Craig Patrick called on old friend Herb Brooks. *(Photo courtesy of the Pittsburgh Penguins)*

"The guy at the station said, 'Hey, there's a phone call,'" Brooks said. "I said, 'Who in the heck knows I'm here, other than my wife?'"

Brooks had been out of coaching for eight years. He returned intent on allowing his star players to be creative.

That was nothing new. While coaching the New York Rangers, he said of flashy forward Pierre Larouche, "Having Pierre Larouche check is like having Picasso paint a garage."

1980 ALL OVER AGAIN

From a marketing standpoint, it was a no-brainer.

Sports Illustrated had named the 1980 U.S. Olympic victory over the Soviet Union—the "Miracle on Ice"—the top sporting moment of the 20th Century, and the Penguins just happened to employ the two architects of that team: coach Herb Brooks and general manager Craig Patrick (who was Brooks' assistant in 1980).

Vice president of marketing, Tom McMillan, arranged for a special ceremony before a game midway through the 2000-01 season, as the 20th anniversary of the miracle on ice approached.

SI hadn't yet made a formal presentation to anyone involved, and Mario Lemieux's good friend, Mike Eruzione—a 1980 Olympic hero—agreed to participate.

It all seemed so perfect, except for one big problem: Brooks wanted no part of it. He thought his European players (and there were many) would be insulted, and he didn't want to draw attention to himself.

Brooks raged and threatened to not show up for the game.

This was like 1980 all over again, with the volatile and unpredictable Brooks running the show.

"Now you know what it was like," Eruzione joked to McMillan.

McMillan was mortified, because Brooks was his sports idol. Finally, McMillan went to Patrick and decided to cancel the production. Lemieux stepped in and ordered it to proceed.

It was a beautiful ceremony. A dramatic, 10-minute video brought tears to people's eyes. Players and fans were riveted.

Brooks wasn't.

He folded his arms on the bench and stared at the floor. He refused to look at the Jumbotron.

"I was sweating like crazy," McMillan said. "I thought, 'We better not fall behind early, and we better not lose, because he'll go to the press conference and blame the ceremony.'"

The Penguins won, and McMillan got a voicemail message from Brooks later that night.

"Tom, I apologize," Brooks said. "It wasn't that bad."

DOG DAYS

Coach Herb Brooks missed a practice for a very unusual reason one day.

Brooks lived out of a hotel during his six-month tenure as Penguins coach. Goaltender J.S. Aubin lived nearby. One day, Brooks was taking a stroll when he spotted Aubin and his girlfriend walking their dog.

As Brooks reached down to pet the dog, his back went out.

"I said to J.S., 'Your dog jumped on me, pushed me, and my back went out, so it's a lawsuit,'" Brooks said the next day, laughing. "I'm going to call your agent."

HERBIE GOES NUTS

Before Herb Brooks came along, Bob Berry was the Penguins' undisputed champion of coaching tirades.

Brooks snatched the crown on January 13, 2000, when he engaged Colorado Avalanche television broadcasters Peter McNab and John Kelly after a 4-3 loss at Colorado.

The exchange occurred in a corridor at the Pepsi Center, near the Penguins dressing room, roughly 15 minutes after the game.

Brooks had just seen a replay of an unpenalized cross check by Colorado's Alexei Gusarov, who hit Penguins winger Matthew Barnaby in the back of the neck with 27.4 seconds left.

Brooks took exception to the fact that Kelly, son of late and legendary St. Louis Blues play-by-play man Dan Kelly, said, "Barnaby has a tendency to embellish," as Barnaby lay on the ice injured.

After Brooks' brief but animated exchange with McNab, Kelly walked past.

Brooks: "Hey, did you make that call on Barnaby?"

Kelly: "What's that?"

Brooks: "Did you say he has a tendency to embellish, when he's down on the ice? Was that your call?"

Kelly: "Herb, do you want to talk about it?"

Brooks: "Was that your call? Was that your call? Was that your call? Was that your call? You say he has a tendency to embellish? He almost tore his head off; he could have killed him. And you said, 'He has a tendency to embellish.' You've got a long way to go to live up to your father's reputation after a cheap shot like that! Did you get a [expletive] life-long contract here? I can't believe that."

Kelly: "That's my opinion, Herb."

Brooks: "That's your opinion? Well, it's a [double expletive] opinion, you understand? Get your [double expletive] out of here!"

Kelly: "You're not going to kick me out of here."

Brooks: "I'll kick your [butt] all over the place, all right? (Brooks pushed Kelly, and the two were separated by an NHL security man). Cheap shot. Has a tendency to embellish. I can't believe that, Kelly. I can't believe that. Go look at the tape."

• • •

Two days later in Nashville, Brooks found out the NHL had suspended him two games.

Between the time he learned of the suspension and spotted a reporter on the street, he was approached by a beggar.

"What did you say to him, Herb?" the reporter asked.

"I gave him $5 and said, 'I'm having a little trouble myself today.'"

WRIGHT WAS WRONG

Tyler Wright wasn't a big-time scorer by any means, but if he'd listened to equipment manager Steve Latin, he would have had a hat trick one night. Wright went into the third period against Carolina with two goals and no edge on his skates.

Latin offered to sharpen them five minutes into the period. Wright declined. Moments later, he had the puck on his stick and an open net in his sights.

He fell down because he lost the edge on his blades.

"I guess I should have listened to the wily veteran," he said.

THE LONGEST GAME

At the end of the fourth overtime, ESPN broadcaster Steve Levy walked over to the writers' section of the press box at Mellon Arena and said, "We're going to be on *ESPN Classic* by the time this is done."

Game 4 of this second-round playoff series, played on May 4, 2000, ended at precisely 12:01 of the fifth overtime, or 2:35 a.m., when Philadelphia's Keith Primeau beat goaltender Ron Tugnutt from the right faceoff circle to give his team a 2-1 victory.

At 152 minutes, one second, it was the third longest NHL game ever played.

Children slept. The press box ran out of beverages. Players took intravenous fluids, changed shirts and pads, and gobbled pizza between periods.

When time stood still: Keith Primeau's goal finally ended it at 12:01 of the fifth overtime, or 2:35 a.m. *(Photo by James M. Kubus/Pittsburgh Tribune-Review)*

Not everybody could stay awake when the Pens and Flyers played five overtimes in the 2000 playoffs. (Photo by James M. Kubus/Pittsburgh Tribune-Review)

"It's certainly hard to describe a game like this," said Penguins coach Herb Brooks. "Where do you start, and where do you finish?"

Start with this: The Flyers were lucky the game went to overtime.

The Penguins held a 1-0 lead when Martin Straka went to the penalty box at 4:47 of the third period. Four seconds later, Flyers winger John LeClair apparently deflected Eric Desjardins' shot past Tugnutt.

The play went to video review to determine whether LeClair tipped the puck with a high stick. Tugnutt and his teammates were positive he had. Replays were inconclusive.

It was a long time before anyone scored again. Eventually, players were skating on fumes.

"You're not even thinking about what you're doing," said Penguins winger Kovalev. "Your body is playing for you."

Among the more remarkable statistics:
- Jaromir Jagr played 59:08.
- Flyers defenseman Dan McGillis led all players by logging 61:05 of ice time.
- Desjardins took 73 shifts.
- Kovalev had 10 shots on goal and missed the net on 10 other attempts.
- Penguins defenseman Peter Popovic blocked nine shots.
- Tugnutt played more minutes (152:01) and made more saves (70) than any goaltender in Penguins' history.
- Flyers goalie Brian Boucher kept the Penguins scoreless for 149:39 after Kovalev's goal at 2:22 of the first period.

The previous longest game in team history occurred April 24, 1996, at Washington, when Petr Nedved beat the Capitals at 79 minutes, 15 seconds of overtime.

Eddie Johnston was on the bench for both games. In the first, he was the Penguins' head coach. In the second, an assistant.

He left with very different feelings the second time, and so did the Penguins, who now found themselves tied in a series they once led two games to none.

They would not win again.

MAN BEHIND THE SCENES

Long after most people had gone home after the third longest game in NHL history, 80-year-old Anthony "A.T." Caggiano was busily working inside the Penguins dressing room.

The Penguins had lost a five-overtime game to the Philadelphia Flyers. The clock read 3:30 a.m.

It proved to be the last game of A.T.'s incredible career. He died 12 days later, saddening the entire Penguins family. A.T. had been involved with Pittsburgh hockey longer than anyone.

Longer, even, than the Penguins' original general manager, Jack Riley.

A.T. started in the 1950s with the old Pittsburgh Hornets of the American Hockey League, and after games, he could be found fishing pucks out of the nets after warm ups, filling water bottles, or performing any of a variety of tasks.

"You could call anybody on any team and they know who A.T. is," said Penguins locker-room attendant Tracy Luppe, "up to and including 'Gretz' [Wayne Gretzky.]"

ROUGH NIGHT

A bunch of weary Penguins returned home from Tokyo in October, 2000, after opening the regular season there with a two-game set against the Nashville Predators.

The team traveled 15 hours on a Monday, arriving home at around 6 p.m. It's hard to imagine anyone's first night was rougher—or stranger—than defenseman Ian Moran's.

"I got home, had a bowl of Golden Grahams, a bagel, two puddings, turned on *Monday Night Football* and woke up with drool all down the front of my T-shirt," he said.

Had Moran's wife not been in Boston, she would have had a premier photo opportunity.

Her husband's night wasn't finished.

"I went upstairs, took a shower, trimmed my beard, fell asleep until around 1, was wide awake from 1 until 4, fell back asleep at 8:30 and slept unbelievable. Woke up again with one of my dogs in the bed and had no idea where I was and what I was doing."

STUNNING NEWS

In late November of 2000, Penguins executive Tom McMillan arranged for what he thought would be a brief, informal meeting with owner Mario Lemieux, who hadn't been seen around the office in a month.

Lemieux's absence was somewhat unusual but didn't raise many eyebrows.

Strangely, though, he called team president Tom Rooney into the office and put his hand up as McMillan began to talk.

"There's been a little change in plans," Lemieux said. "We're going to be moving in a different direction."

Rooney and McMillan, the team's main marketers, feared the worst. Would Lemieux, who had retired three years earlier, relinquish his ownership?

Lemieux leaned forward and said, "I'm coming back."

McMillan remembered waiting for the punch line.

Rooney leaned toward Lemieux and said, "As a player?"

Lemieux, who had been training for the previous month, laughed and said, "Yeah."

"That's when it hit me—he's serious," McMillan said. "It was a surreal situation. I started thinking, 'Everything just changed. All the stuff we've been working on, rip it up.'"

Many details would need to be worked out, particularly the part about Lemieux, then 35, becoming the first full-time sports owner to suit up and play for his team.

But it's not as if the NHL was going to stand in his way.

LEMIEUX DEBUT, PART II

It hardly looked as if Mario Lemieux had gone more than 1,200 days without a competitive game of hockey.

The hockey world stood at attention on December 27, 2000, when Lemieux—already a member of the Hockey Hall of Fame—made his comeback in a home game against the Toronto Maple Leafs. More than 300 press credentials were issued.

Lemieux seemed like an apparition when he raced to center ice at 7:05 p.m. for warmups. The crowd roared at first, then simply stood and watched, as if they couldn't believe what they were seeing.

They roared again when public address announcer John Barbero said, "Add to the Pittsburgh lineup, No. 66, Mario Lemieux."

The lights went down at 7:37 p.m., and Lemieux's No. 66 banner was lowered from the rafters with his four-year-old son, Austin, watching on the ice. Again, the crowd cheered loudly for a moment, then waited.

In their dressing room, the Penguins waited anxiously to take the ice with their 35-year-old owner-turned-player.

"We all tried to talk, but it was weird," defenseman Darius Kasparaitis said. "I hadn't felt that nervous for many years."

As usual, Lemieux delivered the drama.

Seconds into his first shift, he tried his old bank-the-puck-off-the-goalie trick from behind the net. Jaromir Jagr swooped in for the loose puck and tipped it home at the 33-second mark.

The goal stood after a video review. Lemieux had assist No. 882. He finished with a goal and two assists and with the knowledge that his son finally got to see him play in NHL game.

Afterward in the dressing room, Austin Lemieux walked up to his father and said, "I saw you playing. … I saw you."

BLOOD BROTHERS

When Matthew Barnaby was traded from Buffalo to Pittsburgh, everybody asked about his relationship with Sabres enforcer Rob Ray.

Like, why did two close friends want to hit each other so often?

The two had traded punches on golf courses, in watering holes, in locker rooms and at practices.

All in good fun, of course.

Their most publicized clash occurred in the living room of the apartment they shared in Buffalo.

They were watching TV one evening when Ray flicked on the Discovery Channel. Barnaby grabbed the remote control and switched to MTV.

"He ended up going through the Venetian blinds and the screen in the window," Ray said. "It got pretty rough."

A few of Barnaby's teeth found a new address, too.

Not that it soured the friendship.

"What would happen was, we would beat on each other for a while, then we'd go and buy each other beers," Barnaby said. "It was that kind of relationship, one of those brotherly types of things. We'd try to kill each other, but we still liked each other."

FLOOR HOCKEY INCIDENT

Ice hockey wasn't the safest sport for oft-injured Penguins defenseman Janne Laukkanen.

Floor hockey, as it turned out, wasn't much safer.

Laukkanen sustained a torn anterior cruciate ligament one summer as the result of mishaps from a floor hockey game and a wrestling match.

Both events occurred at the bachelor party of Laukkanen's Finnish countryman and former teammate, Sami Salo.

The party was on a small island six hours off the coast of Finland, in the Baltic Sea.

Laukkanen said he injured the knee making a quick stop during a game of floor hockey. Shortly afterward, he twisted the knee during a playful wrestling match.

Both events were alcohol-free, Laukkanen insisted.

UNLUCKY MAN

If he'd walked under a ladder or gotten some bad news from a palm reader, Martin Straka might have understood.

As it was, he couldn't fathom why such an incredible string of bad luck befell him beginning in November of 2001.

First, Straka sustained a broken right leg in a game against the Florida Panthers. Four months later, he returned to the lineup against the Los Angeles Kings, and on his second shift sustained a broken orbital/sinus bone when goalie Johan Hedberg inadvertently struck him with his goal stick.

Martin Straka's unfathomable run of bad luck began with a broken leg on October 28, 2001. *(Photo by James M. Kubus/Pittsburgh Tribune-Review)*

"He's not the luckiest guy on our team," Hedberg allowed.

Straka could have called it quits for the season, but like some character out of a Monty Python movie, he returned a few weeks later against the Carolina Hurricanes.

On his sixth shift, he whiffed on a pass and caught his skate in a rut, re-opening the crack in his leg.

It would get worse.

Straka was at home training in the Czech Republic that summer, two days away from skating again, when he was attacked by a 300-pound barbell.

A weight machine shifted, causing Straka to lose his grip on the barbell. He fell and was pinned under the barbell. Teammate Milan Kraft pulled him from the wreckage.

Straka sustained a chipped vertebra and ligament damage in his back. He feared season-ending surgery but escaped that fate and resumed his career early that season.

Not before one more scare, though.

He was skating laps during a morning workout when—incredibly—he ran into Hedberg's stick again.

The twist was that Hedberg was neither holding the stick nor anywhere near it. It was sitting atop the net. Straka left the ice bleeding.

That night, Straka, sporting a band-aid on his forehead, saw a reporter approaching him.

"Stay away from me," he joked. "Something bad might happen."

JESSE JAMES

Philadelphia Flyers defenseman Luke Richardson outraged Penguins fans in Game 5 of a 2000 playoff series, when he blasted a puck from relatively short range at Penguins defenseman Bob Boughner, striking him in the chest.

Boughner, who was wrestling Flyers forward Keith Jones, went down like he'd been shot.

Penguins coach Herb Brooks verbally tore into Richardson the next day.

"I'd go back in his family tree," Brooks said. "Maybe he's a direct descendant of the guy that shot Jesse James in the back. You know, the coward that shot Jesse James in the back. It must be in his family tree. There's a code for tough guys in the league. This was way past the code."

WHO'S THE WHITE-HAIRED GUY?

Former Penguins coach Ivan Hlinka, a native of Czechoslovakia, had so much trouble communicating with his players that he let assistant coach Rick Kehoe do most of the talking.

One night in Minnesota, defenseman Marc Bergevin decided to play a joke on Hlinka, who could often be found smoking a cigarette near the Zamboni machine between periods and after games.

Bergevin went up to a security guard and said, "The white-haired guy who is outside smoking, he's not with us."

The security guard approached Hlinka and said, "Excuse me, sir, you have to leave."

Replied Hlinka: "Why?"

Security guard: "You can't be here. You gotta go."

Hlinka: "I'm the coach."

Ivan Hlinka was the first Czech-born, NHL coach.
(Photo by James M. Kubus/Pittsburgh Tribune-Review)

Security guard: "No, no, you have to go."

The guard finally gave in, only because players began laughing uncontrollably.

BONE CRACKER

When fearless shot-blocker Ian Moran broke a bone in his right foot on December 10, 2001, it really wasn't anything new.

It simply raised the total of broken bones in his feet to seven in five years.

"Throw in my hands, and I've broken nine bones in five years blocking shots," he said.

Moran almost suffered something much worse than a broken bone a month earlier at the Savvis Center in St. Louis.

A puck headed for his head had "career-ending" written all over it, mostly because the man who launched it was defenseman Al MacInnis, proud owner of one of the hardest shots in NHL history.

"I was legitimately scared for my life," Moran said. "I swear to God, everything just slowed down."

Luckily, the puck hit Moran in the left triceps, then ricocheted off his "teeth or neck or something" and hit teammate Darius Kasparaitis in the chest.

It ultimately wound up on the stick of Blues forward Doug Weight, who pushed it into an open net. Moran wasn't pleased about that but was quite glad to be alive and breathing.

MOOSE ON THE LOOSE

The 27-year-old goalie with the blue mask was thought to be a throw in when the Penguins made an apparently minor trade with the San Jose Sharks on March 12, 2001.

Within weeks, Johan "Moose" Hedberg was a folk hero.

In his debut, he stopped Florida Panthers star Pavel Bure on two of three breakaways—and it was all uphill from there.

Hedberg's mask featured a big blue moose head. His previous team was the minor-league Manitoba Moose.

Incredibly, Hedberg took the Penguins all the way to the Eastern Conference final against the New Jersey Devils, outdueling Olaf Kolzig and Dominik Hasek along the way.

An old Penguin named Olie Sundstrom had helped Hedberg to develop his puck-handling skills back in Sweden (the two used to

Fans went wild over Johan "Moose" Hedberg's playoff heroics in 2001.
(Photo by James M. Kubus/Pittsburgh Tribune-Review)

watch video of Philadelphia's Ron Hextall), and former Penguins defenseman Randy Carlyle coached him in the minor leagues.

Penguins fans wore foam antlers to playoff games that season.

UNLIKELY HERO

The Penguins' second-round playoff series against the Buffalo Sabres in 2001 went to overtime in Game 7.

If somebody had gone into the Penguins dressing room at the point and picked the most unlikely player to score, defenseman Darius Kasparaitis would have been near the top of the list.

Kasparaitis had one goal in 56 playoff games.

But, sure enough, a little more than halfway through the period, he took a pass from Robert Lang at the edge of the left circle and ripped a wrist shot toward legendary goaltender Dominik Hasek.

It went in.

"I can't believe I did that," Kasparaitis said later.

The moment the puck hit twine, Kasparaitis sprinted to center ice and did a belly flop, kicking his legs in the air like an Olympic swimmer.

"I usually kick my feet when I get hurt," he said. "The last time I did it was when I got hit with the puck in the face."

Players were in shock in a delirious Penguins dressing room.

"I haven't seen him score a goal in practice since I've been here," said veteran winger Kevin Stevens, who had rejoined the team three months earlier in a trade. "He's got the worst wrist shot in hockey."

QUOTABLE

Like his Finnish forebearer Ville Siren, Ville Nieminen was a deliciously quotable Penguin. As teammate Randy Robitaille put it, "He always had something to say."

Often, it was something worth pondering, if only for a few seconds.

A sampling of Nieminen-isms:

- On a stretch of good play: "Let's not go building any kind of cloud homes or skyscrapers or something like that. It's just two games."
- On chatting up opponents: "I don't know how they could understand my language. It's Finglish."
- On his stretch of minus games: "Playing like that—having a green jacket at minus-11—is unacceptable."
- On Alexei Kovalev's pinpoint shot that beat Buffalo one night: "You don't even want to celebrate on a goal like that. That was from somewhere else. That guy comes out of some other league, some better league."
- On losing Kovalev in a trade: "There's a hole in the highway. Every player has to chip in a little bit of sand from his own pocket, so we can fill it and keep going."

TRICKS AND TREATS

Rick Kehoe's coaching debut on October 16, 2001, was notable on a few counts.

The Penguins beat Ottawa, 5-2, to avoid becoming the first team in franchise history to open a season with five consecutive losses.

And it proved to be the greatest night of Toby Petersen's career.

Petersen had spent most of his time in the minor leagues and would return there, but on this night he got to play on Mario Lemieux's right wing.

Wearing Kehoe's old No. 17, Petersen scored a hat trick. On his second goal, he took a perfect feed from Lemieux, who froze goalie Patrick Lalime by holding the puck until the very last instant.

"By the time I got the puck, I had a wide-open net," Petersen said. "I pretty much couldn't miss unless my stick broke."

BROKEN GLASS

Left winger Ville Nieminen arrived at training camp in 2002 in excellent shape.

Well, except for those nasty scars on his arms and legs.

Nieminen nearly saw a summer's worth of training go down the drain — literally — when he fell through a sauna door at his home in Finland.

A loose stair caused Nieminen to slip. He crashed legs-first through the sauna's glass door.

"The big door was in 50,000 little pieces," he said. "It looked like somebody got killed in the sauna. There was so much blood that I passed out and hit my face in the glass."

Just before he passed out, Nieminen yelled to his girlfriend to call for help. Luckily, they lived next door to a firehouse.

Help arrived in less than a minute.

"It's a good place to live," Nieminen said.

Doctors needed 62 stitches to close wounds on Nieminen's legs, quadriceps, elbows and forehead.

He escaped debilitating injury and was ready for training camp.

HOCKEY REVOLUTION

Mario Lemieux's impact on Pittsburgh's hockey culture is perhaps best measured by the proliferation of indoor rinks.

When he arrived as a rookie in 1984, the area held just eight rinks, two of which were used year-round. A little more than a decade later, the number approached 30, virtually all of them year-round facilities.

SILENT PENGUIN

Swedish defenseman Hans Jonsson might have been the quietest Penguin, not to mention the most polite toward reporters.

"He doesn't say a word," said Marc Bergevin, Jonsson's former defense partner. "One time I heard his voice. He got hit by a puck. He was moaning."

In the dressing room Jonsson was easy to spot in his trademark blue socks. When approached by a reporter he would dutifully answer questions—often in three words or less—then look the reporter in the eyes and say, "Thank you."

Jonsson played with the Penguins from 1999-2003. Not bad for a guy who was picked last (286th overall) in the 1993 draft and didn't play his first NHL game until he was 26.

Jonsson's teammates would spend valuable time teaching him the nuances of English curse words. They taught him phrases he could use in public, too.

"He learned the phrase hanging in there," teammate Ian Moran said. "So you would say, 'Hans, how are you?' He would say, 'Hanging in there.'"

HOMETOWN HERO

One of Greg Malone's truly memorable games as a Penguins centerman occurred on December 1, 1979, the day his first son, Ryan, was born.

Greg brought his wife, Diana, to the hospital on a Friday night. Their baby wasn't delivered until 4 p.m. Saturday.

With a game scheduled that night, Greg went straight from the delivery room to the arena.

"Our coach, Johnny Wilson, said, 'You want to play?'" Malone recalled. "I said, 'Sure.' During introductions, they said, 'We'd like to welcome the newest Penguin, Ryan Gregory Malone.'"

Approximately 23 years later, PA announcer John Barbero would call Ryan Gregory Malone's name again—every time he scored a goal as a Penguins rookie.

His dad, who had long since become the Penguins' head scout, heard a few of those calls from the press box.

In the 2003-04 season, Ryan Malone became the first Pittsburgh-born and trained player to reach the NHL. And he did it for his hometown team. He wore his dad's old No. 12 and became the first Penguins rookie to score 20 goals since Shawn McEachern in 1992-93.

"These games are like a dream come true for me," he said.

Ryan finished the year with 22 goals and 43 points, Impressive stuff, but he had a way to go to catch up to his old man on the team's all-time scoring list.

Greg Malone was 11th at the time, with 364 points (143 goals, 221 assists). He also shared the team record for assists in a game (six) with Mario Lemieux and Ron Stackhouse.

A child shall lead them: Penguins center Greg Malone and wife, Diana, hold future rookie sensation, Ryan Malone, at a team Christmas party in 1981.
(Photo courtesy of the Pittsburgh Penguins)

• • •

Ryan Malone's game is not very similar to his father's. The two don't share the same view on tattoos, either.

Ryan has the family crest tattooed on his back and a hornet (for his midget team) on his right arm. On his left arm is a dream catcher with Chinese words saying "Follow your dreams," and a Celtic cross with a green dragon, for good luck.

"He knows I don't like 'em, but it's a fad nowadays," Greg Malone said. "Basically, all young people have them. I'm still allowed to make my stand, though."

MY LEFT FOOT

Twice in their history, the Penguins drafted first overall. The first time, in 1984, they took a special, French-Canadian athlete named Mario Lemieux.

The second time, in 2003, they snagged French-Canadian goaltender Marc-Andre Fleury, who proved his incredible athleticism shortly after the draft, during a pool party at general manager Craig Patrick's house.

Fleury was reclining on a raft in the pool when somebody tossed him a miniature plastic ball.

He caught it with his left foot.

DEATH OF A LEGEND

The hockey world mourned on August 11, 2003, when Herb Brooks died in a one-car accident in his home state of Minnesota. He was 66.

"Herb Brooks is synonymous with American hockey, and those of us lucky enough to be around him learned something from him every day," said Penguins general manager Craig Patrick. "I knew him for more than 30 years. We played together, we coached together, and we worked together. Herbie loved the game, he lived the game, and his contributions to the Penguins over the past eight years have been immeasurable. He will be sorely missed."

Throughout his career, Brooks was intensely interested in spreading his hockey knowledge. Penguins coach Eddie Olczyk, a Chicago native who played on the 1984 U.S. Olympic team, will never forget his last encounter with Brooks.

Goalie Marc-Andre Fleury, drafted first overall in 2003, represents the latest in the Penguins' long line of French-Canadian prodigies.
(Photo by James M. Kubus/Pittsburgh Tribune-Review)

It occurred in Pittsburgh a month before Brooks's death, during the Penguins' rookie orientation camp.

Olczyk had just been named Penguins coach.

"One of the last things Herbie said to me was, 'Always remember that you're American-born—you can do it and do it your way,'" Olczyk said. "That's one thing I'll take with me."

6

THE NEXT ONE

Sidney Crosby's Amazing Rookie Year

WINNING TICKET

On the morning of July 22, 2005, Pittsburgh Penguins general manager Craig Patrick made sure to stop by the majestic St. Patrick's Cathedral on Madison Avenue in Manhattan. Couldn't hurt, you know?

Patrick's team had only a 6.25-percent chance of winning the NHL's Draft Lottery later that day. Only three other teams—the Columbus Blue Jackets, the New York Rangers, and the Buffalo Sabres—had as good a chance, but 6.25 percent isn't good under any circumstance. The winning ticket would give a team the right to draft 17-year-old center Sidney Crosby, the NHL's most-celebrated prospect since Mario Lemieux 21 years earlier. By this time, Lemieux was the Penguins' owner.

Back at the Penguins' media room in Mellon Arena, reporters and team employees gathered to watch the lottery on closed-circuit television. In New York, NHL Commissioner Gary Bettman would open 30 envelopes, each with a team logo inside. The 30th would contain the logo of the winning team.

The scene in both venues intensified as Bettman opened envelope Nos. 10, 9, 8, 7, 6, 5, 4 and 3. Only the Penguins and the Mighty Ducks of Anaheim were left. The next envelope held the emblem of the runner-up and thus would give away the winner. Patrick clutched a tiny four-leaf clover—anything to please the Hockey Gods—as Bettman revealed the second-place logo.

It was a Duck.

The roar from Mellon Arena could be heard all the way to Cole Harbour, Nova Scotia, home of Crosby, the kid who'd scored 120 goals and 183 assists in 121 games of junior hockey. He would make his NHL debut on October 5, which happened to be Lemieux's 40th birthday.

LIKE HOTCAKES

Crosby's impact was felt within minutes of the team winning the lottery. Mellon Arena phone lines lit up like Times Square, and ticket-office operators were asked to stay until midnight. A few days later, somebody from Australia called to order seats. By mid-August, the team had sold more tickets than in the entire previous season. This before they even launched their season-ticket marketing campaign. When single-game tickets went on sale, more than 10,000 were sold in four hours, tripling the normal first-day total.

CRYSTAL BALL

Shortly after NHL commissioner Gary Bettman opened the winning envelope on lottery day, Penguins announcer Mike Lange, who was at home, calmly prepared to check the Internet to see who'd won. Just then, a friend called and told Lange the great news: Sid "The Kid" was coming to Pittsburgh.

Lange claimed he wasn't surprised, despite the Penguins having had only a 6.25-percent chance.

"I knew it was going happen," Lange said. "I really did. It isn't something I haven't been saying for the past four or five months. I think it was destiny."

NO SLEEPOVERS

Lots of people expected Crosby to be Mario Lemieux's linemate. Very few expected him to be Lemieux's housemate. Much to the Lemieux's surprise, Crosby moved into the second floor of their suburban mansion and stayed for his entire rookie season. He and Lemieuxs' oldest son, nine-year-old Austin, hit it off, playing hockey in the driveway.

As for house rules, Lemieux said it was perfectly fine for Crosby to have girls over—with one stipulation:

"No sleepovers," Lemieux said.

Sidney Crosby makes a happy arrival in Pittsburgh, with new teammate and future landlord Mario Lemieux standing behind him. *(Photo by James M. Kubus/Pittsburgh Tribune-Review)*

Crosby's reaction?

"No comment," he said, laughing.

And would Crosby, in fact, be required to babysit Mario and Nathalie Lemieux's four young children?

"It's not in his contract," Lemieux said. "But you never know."

FIRST IMPRESSION

A small sampling of hockey fans and Penguins employees got their first live glimpse of the 5-foot-11, 193-pound Crosby in action during an intrasquad scrimmage at training camp. He didn't disappoint.

One look at the faces of men who'd been playing and watching hockey all their lives told the story. Kevin Stevens, a Penguins star turned scout, laughed and shook his head when appraising Crosby's talent.

"Two steps and he's gone," Stevens said. "He's like a Russian-style skater."

Michel Therrien, who was coaching the Penguins' farm team at the time but soon would replace Eddie Olczyk behind the Penguins bench, said, "I sit here in my seat like a fan when that kid's on the ice."

Bob Errey, the Penguins' television analyst, said simply, "He's one of the best passers I've ever seen." That was obvious when Crosby took a feed from John LeClair in the slot and feigned to shoot. Most players would have, but Crosby slid a sweet pass to Mark Recchi for a tap-in.

Recchi was one of the many former Penguins Stanley Cup winners at Mellon Arena that day. Others included, in various on- and off-ice capacities, Mario Lemieux, Stevens, Troy Loney, Phil Bourque, Errey, and assistant coaches Randy Hillier and Joe Mullen.

They all liked what they saw.

MR. POPULAR

Crosby arrived in the NHL with more endorsement opportunities than most players amass in a career, easily surpassing his $850,000 base salary with money made off the ice.

"He's like God north of the border," said Len Rhodes, the Montreal-based vice president of Global Marketing for Reebok Hockey, which signed Crosby to a multiyear deal. "And I know he'll be big south of the border."

Before Crosby set foot in training camp, Reebok had sold more than 16,000 of his No. 87 jerseys. (Crosby wears that number because his birth date is 8/7/87.) What's more, Crosby's Web site, www.crosby87.com was absorbing more than 100,000 hits per day, and he was pitching Gatorade, Reebok, Telus—one of Canada's leading telecommunications companies—and Sherwood. He'd already guest-starred on *The Tonight Show with Jay Leno*. He had appeared shirtless in *Vanity Fair* and fully clothed in *GQ* too.

Another measurement of Crosby's crazy popularity: a Team Canada jersey he'd worn in the gold medal game at the World Junior Championships was stolen, then recovered and auctioned off for $22,100. Proceeds went to youth hockey charities and south Asian tsunami relief.

Reebok knew it was taking a chance on signing an unproven player.

"It's rare for us," Rhodes told the *Pittsburgh Tribune-Review*. "We'd only do it with someone of his caliber."

Crosby's agent, Pat Brisson, said his client took an ardent interest in the marketing realm, right down to the color of the items in Crosby's Reebok clothing line. All items are emblazoned with a SC87 icon, reflecting Crosby's initials and jersey number.

BIG SHOTS

Crosby's rookie deal with Reebok was worth a reported $2.5 million. Some predicted he'd be as big in Pittsburgh as Steelers quarterback Ben Roethlisberger, who made about $4 million off the field in his rookie season.

Getting mentioned in select company was nothing new to Crosby. Soon he would begin shooting ads for Reebok's "I Am What I Am" campaign, which included tennis star Andy Roddick, basketball star Allen Iverson, rapper 50 Cent, actress Christina Ricci, and baseball star Curt Schilling.

Not that Crosby was obsessed with marketing himself. Far from it.

"It'd be nice if the Roethlisberger thing happened to me, but I'm not worried about it," he said. "I can't get caught up worrying about other things besides hockey. I guess in a way, [marketing] is part of it. But I'm here to play hockey."

NO CREDIT

It is easy to forget that Crosby was only 17 when the Penguins drafted him. He didn't turn 18 until a month before training camp. In light of that, it makes a little more sense that he didn't know what to do with his first professional paycheck.

"I haven't seen it yet," Crosby said a few days after it was issued. "I haven't got a bank account, so I'm working on it."

Actually, he had an account back home in Cole Harbour, Nova Scotia, but hadn't yet transferred it. He didn't yet have a credit card yet, either, but soon would have all that and more, including his first vehicle—a leased Range Rover.

LIGHTS, CAMERA, ACTION

Normally, there isn't a news conference at the visiting team's hotel the day before a regular-season opener. But sure enough, the NHL arranged for Crosby and Mario Lemieux to meet the press a day before the Penguins played in New Jersey to kick off the 2005-06 season.

The Kid's debut was that big.

There aren't usually 175 media credentials issued for a regular-season game, either. That's the going number for a conference final, but there were approximately that many issued for this one.

Among the outlets covering Crosby's debut were *Newsweek*, *ET Canada*, and Global TV—a Halifax-based company that rarely covers sports but was on hand to follow native son Crosby.

"We've been covering him since he was 12," said Gray Butler, a cameraman for Global TV. "We're covering this as a news event, not a sporting event. It's about the rebirth of the NHL and about Sidney with the world on his shoulders."

Crosby recorded his first NHL point midway through the third period on a perfect pass across the goalmouth to Mark Recchi. In the opening minutes of the game, Devils goalie Martin Brodeur thwarted Crosby's first NHL shot, a point-blank backhander.

"As much as you'd like to score, you look who's in net, and it's Brodeur who just stopped you," Crosby said after a 5–1 loss. "So you just shake your head a little bit."

PARENT TRAP

About seven hours before his NHL debut, Crosby encountered a most unusual sight as he made his way from the dressing room to the team bus after the morning skate at Continental Airlines Arena.

"There's my parents," he said to a teammate, "in that scrum over there."

Indeed, Troy and Trina Crosby had been engulfed by separate packs of reporters. Somebody asked Troy about his son's recent appearance in *Vanity Fair* magazine.

"Pretty neat," he said. "People said he looked like me a little bit, so it's good."

HOME COOKIN'

Pop diva and Pittsburgh native Christina Aguilera was the surprise anthem singer at Crosby's first home game, thrilling the sellout crowd of 17,132 at Mellon Arena. Crosby made sure the thrills kept coming. At 18:32 of the second period, he scored his first NHL goal, whacking a Mark Recchi pass behind Boston Bruins goaltender Hannu Toivonen.

Fans broke into chant of "Croz-bee! Croz-bee!" after public address announcer John Barbero said, "The Pittsburgh goal . . . scored by No. 87, Sidney Crozbeeee!"

"I was happy," Crosby said. "It's something you dream about, scoring your first NHL goal. You only do it once." He finished with three points in a 7–6 overtime loss.

CANADIAN SHOOTOUT

The first shootout in Montreal Canadiens history doubled as Crosby's official "Here-I-am" moment in Pittsburgh. Every person, it seemed, among the crowd of 16,254 at Mellon Arena on November 10, 2005, stood and cheered after neither team scored in the five-minute overtime. That meant it was time for a shootout. The score was 2–2. Shootouts were new to the NHL in 2005-06, and not surprisingly, proved to be wildly popular. It's hard to dislike a breakaway contest.

Canadiens goaltender Jose Theodore stopped Mark Recchi and Mario Lemieux on the Penguins' first two attempts. Penguins goalie Jocelyn Thibault turned away Michael Ryder, Alex Kovalev, and finally, Alexander Perezhogin to set the stage for Crosby, who took off toward Theodore with a chance to win the game.

The scene was scripted perfectly. Crosby faked a forehand, then planted a missile-like backhander under the crossbar. The water bottle that had been propped atop the net flew high into the air and settled

Sidney Crosby shows off the puck from his first NHL goal, on November 10, 2005 against the Canadiens. *(Photo by James M. Kubus/Pittsburgh Tribune-Review)*

to the ice like ticker tape. The arena shook like it hadn't since the 2001 playoffs.

Pittsburgh, meet your next superstar. Montreal, eat your heart out.

"Montreal was my favorite team growing up," Crosby said afterward. "I feel pretty lucky."

OFF TO SEE THE WIZARD

Pittsburgh native Donald "Dee" Rizzo had never scouted a 13-year-old hockey player before, but an associate from Toronto suggested he take a look at one Sidney Crosby, star center for the Major Midget Dartmouth Subways in Cole Harbour.

"I was embarrassed going to watch a 13-year-old," Rizzo recalled. "I felt like putting on sunglasses. The pathetic thing was, I wasn't the only agent in the building."

Crosby, as usual, dazzled that day. Rizzo immediately reported his find to his partner in Pittsburgh, Steve Reich—agent for Mario Lemieux. Rizzo could barely contain himself in describing this young "Wizard of Croz."

Reich was skeptical. "At that point, it sure sounded ludicrous," he said. "But you know what? It sure doesn't now." It wasn't long before just about every agency in the world wanted a piece of Crosby. Rizzo and another partner, Pat Brisson, beat them all.

RAGE AND FURY

If there were any doubts about Crosby's competitive fire, they were put to rest November 16, 2005, in Philadelphia—a city where the Penguins had been intimidated many times, where they'd once gone 14 years without a victory, and where their all-time record was 17-81-8.

On this night, the Flyers' 6-foot-5, 225-pound monster defenseman, Derian Hatcher, targeted the Penguins' 18-year-old star. At 14:01 of the second period, Hatcher hammered Crosby with a high stick and forearm that broke three of Crosby's teeth. Crosby briefly left the game only to be cracked with another Hatcher high stick—this one across the neck—upon his return.

Hatcher wasn't penalized on either play. Crosby, however, was assessed an unsportsmanlike conduct for complaining. The combination of that call and Hatcher's hits lit a fuse. When Crosby came out for the third period, he skated as if a rocket pack were attached to his back. The Kid assisted on a goal and scored another to stake the Penguins to a 2–0 lead. The Flyers tied it with two late power-play goals, but Crosby won it on a breakaway with 46.7 seconds left in overtime.

When puck hit twine, Crosby, still at full speed, circled back toward his bench pumping his arms in celebration. His jersey was stained with blood.

"When stuff like that happens, you maybe try to push a little harder than normal," Crosby said, typically understating the situation. "I just wanted to make sure we got the win. I thought we deserved it."

Crosby's teammates couldn't help but be impressed.

"You see a lot of guys, they'll take one hit, one stick, and they shut it down for the rest of the game," said defenseman Brooks Orpik. "He responded great."

LOOK MA, BROKEN TEETH

It's never wise for a hockey player to get too attached to his teeth. Crosby wasn't. He just didn't expect three of them to be halved in the 21st game of his rookie season, courtesy of a high stick and forearm from Philadelphia Flyers defenseman Derian Hatcher.

Crosby's mother, Trina, was more upset than Crosby.

"She asked, 'Where's your mouthguard?'" Crosby said the next day.

As usual, Crosby had left his mouthguard in his gear bag for that particular game. He didn't plan to start wearing one because of the incident, either. Not all players are as lucky as Penguins television analyst and long-time NHL player Bob Errey, whose original teeth are intact.

Sidney Crosby may have lost some teeth, but the Penguins defeated the Flyers in overtime, 3-2. *(Photo by Jim McIsaac/Getty Images)*

"I'm not too worried about it," said Crosby, who also sustained a cut on his upper lip that required four stitches. "I pretty much realized it was eventually gonna happen. Not 20 games in, but it's happened already, so it's out of the way, and I don't have to worry about it anymore, I guess."

Crosby figured his mom would get over it. Hey, a kid loses all his first teeth. What's the big deal about losing some of the replacements?

"She knows it's part of hockey," Crosby said through a reconfigured smile.

INCREDIBLE FEAT

Crosby was the youngest player in the NHL's 89-year history to reach 100 points, the seventh rookie to hit that mark, and the only rookie to record 100 points and 100 penalty minutes. He finished with 102 points (39 goals, 63 assists) and 110 penalty minutes. He joined Hall of Fame forward Dale Hawerchuk of the Edmonton Oilers (103 points, 1981-82) as the only other 18-year-old to reach 100 points.

Crosby's tender age is what set his rookie year apart from so many others is sports history. Joe Thornton, the 2005-06 NHL scoring champion, had seven points in 55 games as an 18-year-old. Tampa Bay's Vincent Lecavalier had 28 points in 82 games.

NBA star Kobe Bryant averaged 7.6 points when he was 18. Baseball Hall of Famer Robin Yount batted .250. Cleveland Cavaliers star LeBron James put up 20.9 points per game his rookie season, but he turned 19 two months into it.

No one, least of all Crosby, expected a 100-point season. Did he meet his own expectations?

"In a way, to a certain point," he said. "I wanted to come in here and get comfortable right away and adjust as well as I could. I think I did that. But as far as the winning side of it, I don't think I could accept not winning. It's not something I want to get used to. Individually, I was pretty happy with the way things went. But on the other side of it, I want to win.

"I'd probably trade a few of those [points] for some wins and a playoff spot."

BLADE RUNNER

One thing Crosby will never have to worry about is an opposing coach calling for a measurement of his blade.

Crosby uses on old-school stick—a two-piece model with a straight, wooden blade. He said it probably takes something away from his wrist shot. But he doesn't mind, because of how easily he is able to make back-handed passes and snap back-handed shots with more force and accuracy than many players have on their forehand shots.

Penguins equipment manager Steve Latin could scarcely recall a player who used a blade so straight. Ron Francis was one. Most modern players favor one-piece graphite sticks with curved blades.

Crosby said he had no inclination to change. He'd been playing with the same kind of stick all his life and hadn't done too poorly.

"I guess that's the best way to describe it—old-school," Crosby said.

Crosby's game-day superstitions, by the way, include always putting his equipment on the right-hand side first and not allowing anyone to make contact with his stick after it's taped.

Not until the first goal celebration, anyway.

THE NEXT ONE

When Crosby was 15, a reporter from the *Arizona Republic* asked Wayne Gretzky if there was any young player out there who could break his records. "Yes, Sidney Crosby," The Great One replied. "He's the best player I've seen since Mario Lemieux." That statement added some serious fuel to the Crosby legend and led to some labeling him The Next One.

Ironic, then, that Gretzky snubbed Crosby when it came time to choose the 2006 Canadian Olympic team. Crosby didn't complain, but Gretzky, who ran Team Canada, no doubt regretted the move. The veteran-laden Canadian team did not medal in Torino, Italy, and Crosby finished his rookie season third among Canadian-born scorers with 102 points.

Another young player left off the Olympic team, Carolina's Eric Staal, finished the season with 100 points.

WASN'T MEANT TO BE

The Old Man and the Kid. Mario Lemieux and Sidney Crosby. They were supposed to make sweet music together for at least a year, skating on the same power play and perhaps even the same line. When the Penguins won the draft lottery, that was a major part of the story, but it didn't have a happy ending.

The two combined directly on only one goal—albeit a beauty—on November 3 at Nassau Coliseum in Long Island. Lemieux threaded a pass from just inside the blue line that Crosby deflected high into the net for a power-play goal at 4:01 of the third period of a 5–1 victory. It marked the first two-goal game of Crosby's career.

Crosby and Lemieux played in just 26 games together, only a handful of those on the same line. They had points on the same goal only eight times before Lemieux retired in January because of an irregular heartbeat.

At one point during his retirement news conference, Lemieux's eyes welled as he turned to his teammates, 10 of whom were rookies, and said, "All I can say to the young players is, 'Enjoy every moment of it. Your career goes by very quickly.'"

Despite his tender age, Crosby seemed to have an appreciation for Lemieux's words. He lamented the fact that the two shared so little ice together, but added, "It makes us all realize how fortunate we are to be playing."

SLEEP TALKER

Crosby received a New Year's gift when gregarious winger Colby Armstrong was recalled from the minors. The two became fast friends; road roommates; and, eventually, linemates.

Armstrong's sense of humor helped lighten the load on Crosby. Sometimes, that could even mean Armstrong taking a good-natured shot at Crosby's thick lips.

"He has a good sense of humor," Armstrong said. "You can rip on him a little bit, and he takes it really well. He doesn't get too wrapped up in a lot of stuff."

As for Crosby's habits on the road, Armstrong said his roomie likes to stretch a lot, usually goes to bed early—and talks in his sleep.

"He does that quite a bit, talks about hockey," Armstrong said. "The odd time he'll spit something out, and I don't even know what the heck it means. I try to keep it going, talking to him, but he doesn't wake up."

CONSTANT ADVERSITY

Throughout his rookie season, Crosby insisted he had arrived in Pittsburgh without any expectations. Good thing, because they would have been shattered fairly quickly.

Among the unexpected events:

The abrupt retirements of two linemates (Ziggy Palffy and Mario Lemieux)

A coaching change (Michel Therrien replaced Eddie Olczyk after the team's 8-17-6 start.)

A system change

A position change (Olczyk had Crosby playing left wing.)

Lemieux stepping down as team CEO and putting the franchise up for sale

A terrible team (the Penguins finished with the second-worst record in the NHL.)

The firing of Hall of Fame general manager Craig Patrick two days after the season finale in Toronto.

Through it all, Crosby never showed signs of breaking under the pressure. The season ended the way it began—with a media horde surrounding a composed and smiling Crosby.

"I came in pretty open-minded and just tried to go with the flow and enjoy it," he said. "I think sometimes when you expect things you're caught off-guard. A lot of things happened, good and bad. Every season's like that."

But none were quite like this.

CHERRY PICKER

Controversial and immensely popular Canadian hockey analyst Don Cherry has been picking on Crosby for years.

When Crosby scored an incredible goal in the Quebec Major Junior Hockey League—he scooped the puck lacrosse style, rested it on the blade of his stick, and stuffed it into the net—Cherry ripped him on *Hockey Night in Canada*.

"I like the kid," Cherry said. "But this is a hot-dog move."

A year later, Cherry criticized Crosby for skipping a prospects All-Star game, and early in Crosby's rookie year, Cherry accused him of diving. Not long after that, Cherry was at it again, saying it was "ridiculous" that new coach Michel Therrien made Crosby an alternate captain. Cherry also implied that Crosby backed the firing of coach Eddie Olczyk.

"No kid should have as much to say as he's got to say," said Cherry, as reported by the Canadian Press. "Yapping at the referees, doing the whole thing. Golden boy."

Crosby, like millions of Canadians, had spent many a Saturday night watching Cherry during the Coach's Corner segment on *Hockey Night in Canada*. If he was bothered by Cherry's jabs, he didn't let on.

"He's always been opinionated, and I always watch Saturday night to see what he's going to say," Crosby told the *Pittsburgh Tribune-Review*. "In my case, he's mentioned my name probably not in the best of ways, but it is what it is. Everyone's entitled to their opinion. I think everyone can [read the comments] and make their own opinions. That's fine with me."

BUDDING RIVALRY

Back in the early 1980s, the friendly rivalry between Magic Johnson and Larry Bird transformed the NBA, lifting it to new heights of popularity. Someday, perhaps, Crosby and Alexander Ovechkin of the Washington Capitals will become the Johnson and Bird of the NHL.

Crosby and Ovechkin waged a riveting battle for the league's Calder Trophy. Ovechkin finished with 106 points, Crosby with 102. Crosby outscored Ovechkin in the head-to-head matchup, nine points to six, as the Penguins took three of four games.

Both players downplayed the rivalry, but it was obvious in watching the games.

"There's a healthy competition there," Crosby admitted. "I respect him."

GRAND FINALE

No one who was at Mellon Arena on April 17, 2006, will forget the scene. Fans began to line up three hours before the Penguins' final home game of the season, eager for one last look at Crosby, who was three points shy of becoming the youngest player in NHL history to reach 100.

Before the game, the normally cool Crosby turned to teammate Ryan Malone and said, "I haven't been this nervous in a long time."

A standing-room-only crowd of 17,048 roared as if it were Game 7 of the Stanley Cup final, not the last home game for a miserable team that would finish with the second-worst record in the league. Fans nearly blew the roof off the place 1:56 into the game, when Crosby assisted on an Andy Hilbert goal for his 98th point. No. 99 came at 15:19 of the second period. Twenty-five seconds after that, Crosby slipped a pass to Malone for a power-play goal and point No. 100. He was the seventh rookie in league history to reach the milestone.

Bedlam ensued.

Fans waved white T-shirts that read "Pittsburgh First," a reference to the group that was fighting to keep the Penguins in Pittsburgh. Some threw their shirts onto the ice. Penguins general manager Craig Patrick, witnessing his final game from the Mellon Arena press box, openly wept. He would be fired less than a week later.

The scoreboard flashed "Sidsational" then this: "Youngest Player in NHL History to Score 100 Points."

"It was amazing," Crosby said of the fan support. "Once I got those first two, I was just feeding off of them. I knew I couldn't leave here tonight without getting the other one. They were awesome. I'm really happy I was able to do it here."

The feeling was mutual—and the fans couldn't wait for the next chapter of Sidney Crosby's career, for with it would come the next Sidsational moment.

Celebrate the Variety of Pittsburgh-Area Sports
in These Other NEW and Recent Releases from Sports Publishing!

Game of My Life: Penn State
by Jordan Hyman
• 6 x 9 hardcover
• 240 pages
• photos throughout
• $24.95
• 2006 release!

Roberto Clemente: The Great One
by Bruce Markusen
• 6 x 9 hardcover
• 362 pages
• 12-page photo insert
• $22.95

Don Nehlen's Tales from the West Virginia Sideline
by Don Nehlen with Shelly Poe
• 5.5 x 8.25 hardcover
• 192 pages
• photos throughout
• $19.95
• 2006 release!

Pittsburgh Steelers: Men of Steel
by Jim Wexell
• 6 x 9 hardcover
• 220 pages
• 35 b/w photos throughout
• $19.95
• 2006 release!

Tough as Steel: Pittsburgh Steelers – 2006 Super Bowl Champions
by the *Tribune-Review*
• 8.5 x 11 hardcover and softcover
• 128 pages
• color photos throughout
• $19.95 (hardcover)
• $14.95 (softcover)
• 2006 release!

Myron Cope: Double Yoi!
by Don Nehlen with Shelly Poe
• 6 x 9 softcover
• 300 pages
• photo insert
• $16.95
• 2006 release!
• First time available in softcover!

Tales from the Pitt Panthers
by Sam Sciullo Jr.
• 5.5 x 8.25 hardcover
• 200 pages
• photos throughout
• $19.95

Tales from Behind the Steel Curtain
by Jim Wexell
• 5.5 x 8.25 hardcover
• 200 pages
• photos throughout
• $19.95

Roethlisberger: Pittsburgh's Own Big Ben
by Sports Publishing L.L.C.
• 8.5 x 11 softcover
• 128 pages
• color photos throughout
• $14.95

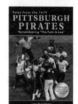

Tales from the 1979 Pittsburgh Pirates: Remembering "The Fam-A-Lee"
by John McCollister
• 5.5 x 8.25 hardcover
• 200 pages
• photos throughout
• $19.95

All books are available in bookstores everywhere!
Order 24-hours-a-day by calling toll-free **1-877-424-BOOK (2665).**
Also order online at **www.SportsPublishingLLC.com.**